Harpers Ferry (looking down and westward from Maryland Heights).

A. Site of Hall's "Rifle Works".
B. Site of "Musket Factory".
C. Site of "Large Arsenal".

Shenandoah River

Potomac River

In the left foreground are the stone abutments of the 1836 railroad bridge destroyed by the Confederates. In the center is the bridge built following the Civil War (and after the arsenal-armory was abandoned). To the right is the bridge presently used by the main line of the Baltimore and Ohio Railroad. The post-Civil War railroad tracks cover much of the area formerly occupied by the arsenal-armory.

The
Guns
of
Harpers Ferry

By

Stuart E. Brown Jr.

CLEARFIELD

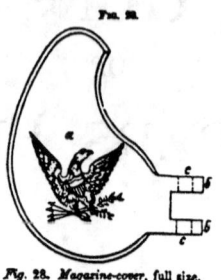

Fig. 28. Magazine-cover, full size.

Copyright © 1968
by
Virginia Book Company
All Rights Reserved.

Reprinted for
Clearfield Company, Inc. by
Genealogical Publishing Co., Inc.
Baltimore, Maryland
1993, 1994, 1996, 1998, 2001, 2002

International Standard Book Number: 0-8063-4640-X

Made in the United States of America

CONTENTS

Foreword	5
The Beginnings at Harpers Ferry	9
I. The Early Muskets	13
Model 1795	13
Model 1795 Musketoon (?)	15
"Model 1808"	18
Model 1812	21
Model 1812 (Artillery)	25
II. The Early Rifles	28
Model 1800 (?)	28
Full Octagonal Barrels and Full Maple Stocks (?)	28
Model 1803	29
Lewis and Clark Rifles	30
Cover Illustration	33
Model 1803 (continued)	35
"Officer's Models"	40
Set Triggers	40
III. The Early Pistols	43
Pistols Pre-Dating the Model 1806 (?)	43
Model 1806	43
Pairs	47
Patterns for North Model 1811 (?)	51
Patterns for North Model 1813	51
Patterns for North Model 1816 (?)	52
Model 1819 (patterns)	53
Model 1836 (patterns) (?)	55
IV. The 1816-1822 Series	57
Model 1816 Musket	57
Model 1822	60
Model 1816 Musket (Artillery)	61
Model 1819 Rifle	65
V. The Hall Arms	69
The Hall Harpers Ferry Receivers	75
Model 1819 Rifle (Hall) (flintlock)	78
Model 1841 Rifle (Hall) (percussion)	79
Harpers Ferry Hall Carbines	81
Model 1834 Carbine (Hall)	81
Model 1840 Carbine (Hall)	83
Rifled Carbines (?)	84
VI. The 1840 Series	87
Model 1840 Musket (model and patterns)	87
Model 1840 Musketoon (model and/or pattern)	89
VII. The 1841-1842 Series (percussion)	93
Model 1841 Rifle ("Mississippi")	93
Model 1842 Musket	97
Musketoon	99

```
VIII. The 1855 Series                                          101
        Model 1855 Rifle                                       103
        Model 1855 Rifle Musket                                107
        Model 1855 Pistol-Carbine                              109
        Model 1855 Rifle Carbine (?)                           110
IX. Miscellaneous                                              113
        Model 1857 Rifle (Navy) ("Plymouth")                   113
        Rampart Rifles                                         115
        Harpoon Guns                                           115
        Blunderbusses                                          124
        1847 Wall Piece (model) ("Sharpshooter's Rifle")       126
        Presentation Pieces                                    126
X. Production Records                                          131
Acknowledgements                                               137
Illustrations Credits                                          139
Short-Title Index                                              141
Bibliography                                                   143
Index                                                          151
Additional Photographs                                     155-157
```

FIRST GREAT SEAL OF THE UNITED STATES

FOREWORD

At Harpers Ferry, the Shenandoah River pours into the upper Potomac, and the combined river, the Potomac, passing through a magnificent gap or hole in the Blue Ridge Mountains, flows eastward to the Atlantic Ocean. Harpers Ferry, originally called "The Hole", takes its latter-day name from a public accommodation owned and operated by early settler Robert Harper (and the possessive apostrophe is generally omitted).

Harpers Ferry was first known as a place of great natural beauty - - - Thomas Jefferson, addressing himself to European readers, wrote in his best selling Notes on the State of Virginia that "the scene (at Harpers Ferry) is worth a voyage across the Atlantic".

Then, in 1792, Congress authorized the establishment of two national arsenals for the storage, etc., of arms; in 1794, it authorized the construction of two national armories for the manufacture of small arms; and President George Washington, combining the two authorizations, selected Springfield, Massachusetts, as the site for the northern arsenal-armory, and the tiny settlement of Harpers Ferry, located on the peninsula lying between the upper Potomac and the Shenandoah, as the site for the southern arsenal-armory. And by the early 1840's, Harpers Ferry was a thriving manufacturing village - - - including suburbs, it had a population of over 3,000. (1)

Harpers Ferry was served by highways, by railroads, and by the Chesapeake and Ohio Canal - - - through it passed the main flow of east-west traffic - - - and to it, in 1859, came John Brown and his men (armed with Sharps carbines) to give to Harpers Ferry a third dimension.

Finally, the Civil War destroyed Harpers Ferry - - - "a place more thoroughly gutted could not be imagined" (2) - - - and thereafter, for many years, ghosts walked its streets.

Today, Harpers Ferry is under the jurisdiction of the National Park Service. The restored Master Armorer's House is now open to visitors, and although much additional restoration remains to be done, Harpers Ferry is well worth a visit.

In addition to firearms, Harpers Ferry produced tons and tons of firearm appendages, accoutrements, spare parts and tools, at least one cannon, a few sword blades, and several thousand "minnie balls" and cartridges. It also altered, fabricated, and repaired thousands and thousands of firearms (and "fabricated" as used in the early part of the 19th Century meant assembled rather than manufactured). But this study will not touch upon any products other than firearms, and it will not attempt to cover the subject of bayonets.

Nor will this study touch upon how and with what materials and machinery the Harpers Ferry firearms were made, or upon who made them, other than to mention here that some of America's great gunmakers are believed to have worked at Harpers Ferry, men such as Henry Hawkins, father of the Hawkens of St. Louis, and Christian Sharps, the producer of the John Brown weapons.

This study will mention only a few of the many official post-production alterations and conversions of the Harpers Ferry firearms. And as regards unofficial alterations and conversions, it will only point out here that a large portion of the firearms produced at Harpers Ferry probably went to the southern states (while a large portion of those produced at Springfield, the northern national arsenal-armory, probably went to the northern states), and recall here that the Confederacy, in her desperate struggle to arm her soldiers, effected many unconventional alterations and conversions.

This study will not neatly classify all of the firearms made at Harpers Ferry, and the probabilities are that no other study will ever do so unless, of course, someone unearths the original records that are believed to have burned in the conflagration of April 18, 1861.

In classifying the firearms made at Harpers Ferry, one can be certain only of the fact that there are many uncertainties, and in attempting to classify unusual Harpers Ferry arms, one must not forget that, during many of Harpers Ferry's years, new firearms were not planned on drawing boards. They evolved, instead, from one or even a series of full-scale models, and Harpers Ferry's close proximity to Washington resulted in the production by Harpers Ferry of myriads of models, experimental arms, etc., as well as numerous patterns.

Colonel B. R. Lewis states that Harpers Ferry maintained a shop for making models, experimental arms, patterns, etc., and he also points out that the Ordnance Department's Regulations of 1834 (the earliest of which he has knowledge) mention a Washington "Model Office", and he advises that it served as a depository for approved models, patterns, etc.; that when guages were used, a complete set was sent to the Model Office, another was sent to each armory, and yet another was sent to the officer responsible for contract arms inspection; and that the Model Office kept a Model Book which contained descriptions of approved models, details of actions of the Ordnance Board, etc. Finally, Colonel Lewis states that "as late as 1942", when the Ordnance Office was located in the Social Security Building, the models, etc., were in existence, being kept in cabinets in the Hall. (3)

This study will not attempt to unravel the mystery of many of the varied marks (letters and numerals) that appear on the firearms made at Harpers Ferry.

Finally, this study will touch only lightly upon where and by whom the Harpers Ferry firearms were used, but mentioning here the probability that, in their day, the Harpers Ferry firearms accompanied the flag wherever it went, and that, not too many years ago, at least one Virginia farmer (a resident of Caroline County) was shooting rabbits with his trusty "Harpers Ferry".

In this study, in an effort to avoid confusion, the shooting end of an arm is called the "front" end, while the opposite end of the arm is called the "rear" end.

Also, since the words "model" and "pattern" tend to overlap, an arm of a new design made for submission to an authority for approval will be called a "model" (with a lower case "m"). If a model was approved, it became the prototype of a Model (with an upper case "M"), e.g., the prototype of the Model 1841 Rifle. Each copy of a prototype that was produced to serve as a guide for a maker will be called a "pattern". And each arm made for regular use will be referred to as a "general issue" arm.

The probabilities are that Harpers Ferry kept, for reference, a duplicate of every model sent out from Harpers Ferry.

Notes

(1) Howe, Historical Collections of Virginia 335-6.
(2) West Virginia. A Guide to the Mountain State 231, quoting David Hunter Strother ("Porte Crayon"), a native of West Virginia's panhandle (which includes Harpers Ferry).
(3) Letter to author. April 15, 1968.

Harpers Ferry ca. 1803. View looking eastward from the heights of Harpers Ferry, and down the Potomac. The Shenandoah River is at the lower right. Drawing by W. Roberts, Esq., engraved by J. Jackes. The building in the center foreground later came to be known as the "Large Arsenal". One of the arsenal-armory's warehouses is shown in the lower left (along the Potomac).

THE BEGINNINGS AT HARPERS FERRY

Harpers Ferry's location was fortuitous. It lay beyond the range of naval gunfire and of amphibious operations. Water power was more than ample - - - Harpers Ferry suffered frequently from floods. In the near vicinity there were skilled workmen - - - the rifle-making sections of Maryland and Pennsylvania lay just to the north, the rifle-making area of the Shenandoah Valley lay just to the west and southwest, and Fredericksburg, an arms-making center during the Revolution, lay not far to the southeast. Also, in the near vicinity, there was coal, iron, and black walnut timber - - - maple may have been used on some of the earliest Harpers Ferry firearms, but otherwise, black walnut was used exclusively. Roughed out stocks were purchased from local private contractors, and a goodly number were kept on hand - - - United States standards set in 1823 provided that "no stocks should be used, which have not been cut from a plank at least three years, and have been stored in a dry place for two years", and that "kiln dried, or steamed stocks, should not be received" (1), and in 1860, for example, Harpers Ferry had an inventory of 130,000 seasoned stocks.

The authorization of the two arsenal-armories was but one step in the process of transforming the loose-knit confederation of colonies into a United States, and, of course, there was a need for firearms. Prior to the Revolution, England supplied arms to the Colonies, and during the Revolution, the Colonies obtained many arms from France, but following the Revolution, England continued to be hostile, and in 1789, France was all but torn apart by her own revolution.

Moreover, in the 1790's, there were dangers aplenty. Spain held Florida as well as the vast trans-Mississippi area known as Louisiana. England held Canada, and used it as a base for supporting the many Indians who were constantly harassing the northwest frontier. And at sea, both France and England were trying to prevent the United States from rising to a position of mercantile and naval prominence.

In 1794, the United States and England finally signed a treaty of peace, but the French Directory, claiming that the treaty violated the Franco-American Alliance of 1778, retaliated by subjecting the United States to a series of studied insults. Striving for harmony, the United States dispatched a delegation to France, but Talleyrand, the French Minister, refused to even receive the United States delegation unless the delegation first paid a large bribe, and committed the United States to loan France a large sum of money. This, the "XYZ Affair", was one insult too many, and on June 18, 1798, in Philadelphia at a dinner honoring John Marshall, the shining light of the United States delegation, Robert Goodloe Harper raised his glass and proposed: "Millions for defense, but not a cent for tribute".

Washington was recalled from retirement at Mount Vernon - - - his new commission was dated July 4, 1798 - - - and that fall, plans were made for his troops to "hut" (i.e., to go into winter quarters) at and in the vicinity of Harpers Ferry.

In the interim, the Harpers Ferry armory-arsenal authorization had apparently dozed, but the war scare or General Washington or both caused it to reawaken, and by September of 1798, Joseph Perkin, a Philadelphia gunmaker, was on the job at Harpers Ferry as Superintendent, and a building program was underway. (2)

A total of $1092.17 charged in 1798 to Harpers Ferry's manufacture of arms account indicates that Harpers Ferry may have produced arms in 1798. (3)

Satterlee states that Harpers Ferry produced arms in 1799 (4), and $9520.49 was charged to the manufacture of arms account in 1799 (5), but apparently, there are no firearms in existence that were made at Harpers Ferry prior to 1800.

- - - - - - - - - - - - - - - - - - -

In 1799, Napoleon became dictator of France, and girding for European wars, he reestablished peace with the United States. This ended the "mad scramble to secure arms to meet the impending crisis", but in 1800, Napoleon forced Spain to cede Louisiana to France, and Louisiana under Napoleon and France was doubly dangerous.

- - - - - - - - - - - - - - - - - -

Harpers Ferry did produce firearms in 1800, a year in which expeditures totalling $11,397,12 were charged to the manufacture of arms account. (6)

Notes

(1) Regulations for the Inspection of Small Arms 4.
(2) Gurney 5.
(3) Ibid.
(4) Satterlee 164.
(5) Gurney. 5.
(6) Ibid.

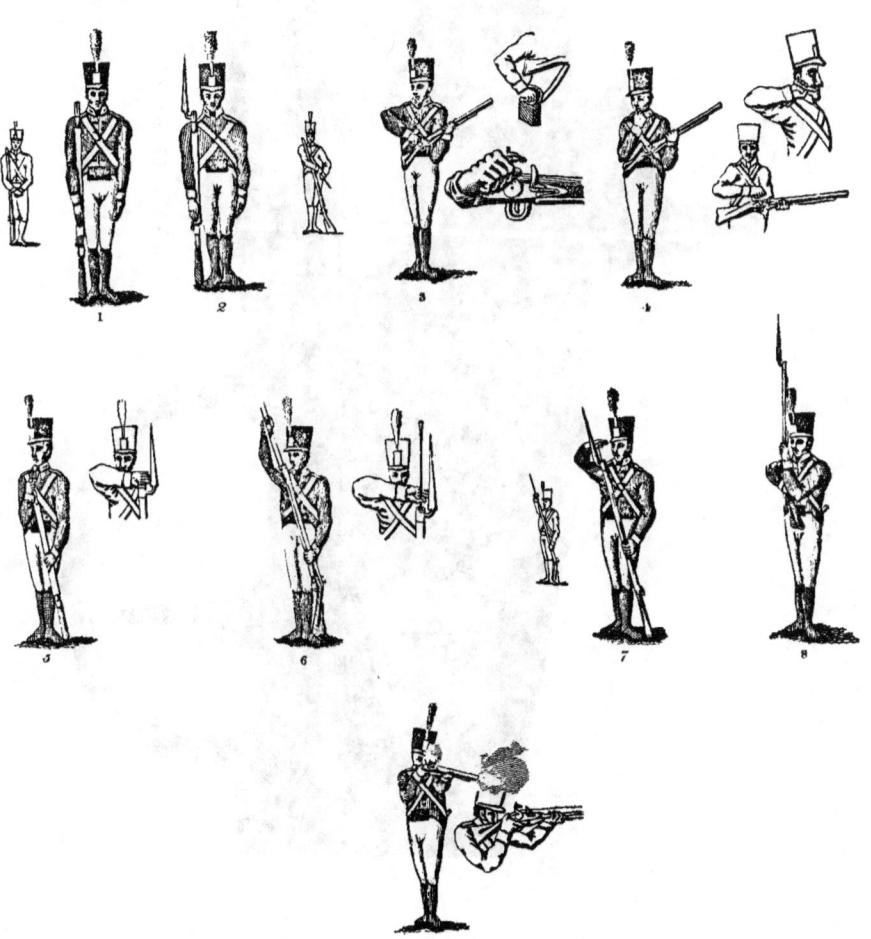

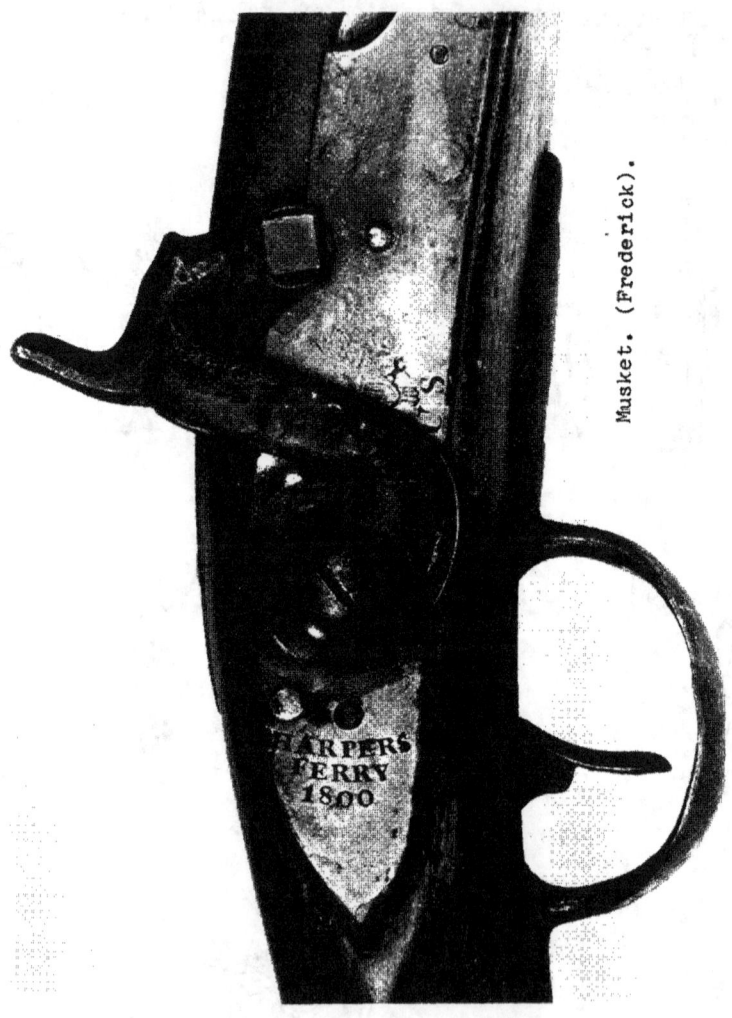

Musket. (Frederick).

I. THE EARLY MUSKETS

One Harpers Ferry musket (converted to percussion, and otherwise altered), with a lockplate dated 1800, is reported as having the early type small butt, and two iron ferrules on the forward end of the stock to hold the tapered wooden ramrod. (1)

Model 1795

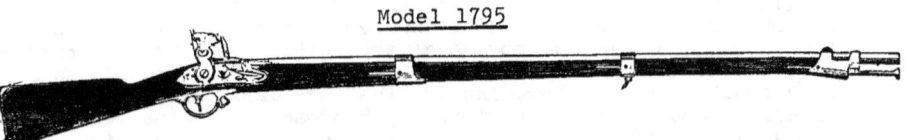

However, the probabilities are that most of the first muskets made at Harpers Ferry were of the same general type as the Colonies' favorite Revolutionary War weapon, the French Model 1763 Musket manufactured at such royal armories as Charleville, Maubeuge, St. Etienne, et al. Since most of the French Model 1763 Muskets used by the Colonies were made at Charleville, the Americans commonly called every French Model 1763 Musket a Charleville ("Charley Ville").

Exact (or nearly exact) copies of the Charleville were made at Springfield as early as 1795, and these, the first muskets produced at Springfield, are labelled, unofficially, Model 1795's. Also, the first muskets produced at Harpers Ferry are usually labelled, unofficially, Model 1795's.

But, apparently, the earliest Harpers Ferry muskets (lockplates dated 1800, et seq.) are not exact (or nearly exact) copies of the Charleville. One exception may be the Harpers Ferry musket, serial number 4845, that is described in part in a dealer's catalogue as follows: "The lock is dated 1811, but it is an exact Charleville pattern, and must have been made earlier than 1811". (2)

The earliest Harpers Ferry muskets are, at the closest, cousins to the Charleville, and cousins to the Springfield Model 1795. It is confusing to refer to them as Model 1795's, but it might be equally confusing to use some other label.

It is also confusing as well as incorrect to equate the pre-1816 Harpers Ferry muskets with the pre-1816 Springfield muskets - - - prior to 1816, the two national armories made no effective efforts to standardize their products.

Moreover, the earliest Harpers Ferry muskets are not twins. They vary, and in the past, in evaluating the variations, a great deal of ink has been shed on whether or not the rear end of a lock plate is tit-like or tit-less, upon whether or not the rear of a comb is curved or straight, upon whether or not the top of a comb is curled, upon whether a flint screw is pierced only or is pierced and slotted, upon whether or not there is a curl in the tail of the frizzen, upon the length of a barrel, upon the length of a stock, upon the shape of a butt, and upon small differences in the size and shape of the bands. However, in considering these variations, most of which are non-functional, one must bear in mind (a) that the period from 1798 to 1816 was troublous, (b) that the moveable parts of the lock had short life expectancies, (c) that materials and manufacturing techniques were constantly changing, and (d) that the early Harpers Ferry firearms were handmade or virtually handmade, with the resulting probabilities that many of the variations reflect the whims, the styles, and even the carelessnesses of individual artisans rather than official, purposeful changes in design.

Nevertheless, the design of the early United States muskets was not static, nor was that of the contemporary French muskets - - - the Charleville was improved in 1766, 1768, 1770, 1771, 1773, 1774 and 1777. (3)

1800 Dated Specimens

A specimen, with an 1800 dated lockplate, and with serial number 2150 marked on the barrel, was reported a number of years ago as being in the collection of Edward Field of Providence, R.I. (4)

A specimen with a lockplate dated 1800 (perhaps the Field specimen) is reported by C. Meade Patterson as having a round bottom pan, as having a comb that is straight (rear), and that does not have a curl at the top, and as not having a curl in the tail of the frizzen. Patterson goes on to state that the specimen "really looks like a U.S. Model 1808 flintlock musket as made at Springfield except that it has the French Model 1763 Charleville trigger guard straps with pointed ends having the tear drop finial". Patterson concludes that Harpers Ferry made this type of musket through the War of 1812. (5)

1802 Dated Specimens

A dealer's catalogue lists a specimen with an 1802 dated lockplate, and with serial number 1331 marked on the barrel. (6)

A specimen with a lockplate dated 1802 is reported as being in the collection of W. M. Robertson. It has a lockplate measuring 6 1/4 in. by 1 3/16 in., and the lockplate markings correspond with those of the Model 1806 Pistols. The rear of the Robertson lockplate is described as ending in a tit-less point.

The Robertson pan, like all of the early Harpers Ferry pans, is forged integrally with the lockplate, and has a fence and a round bottom.

The Robertson cock is plain above the cap, and the tail of the frizzen is plain.

The stock is 57 1/2 in. long, it has a 5/8 in. comb, and the small of the stock does not extend to the butt. The butt plate is marked with serial number 2189.

The Robertson barrel is 45 in. long, it bears serial number 2189 at the breech, and the marks on the top of the barrel correspond with those on the Model 1806 Pistols. Proof marks "V" and "I" are also stamped in the center of the breech. The breech tang measures 2 1/4 in., the breech plug has neither a hole nor a slot for the passage of the rear lock bolt, and on the bottom of the barrel, there is a bayonet stud as well as a turning lug located 4 1/4 in. from the muzzle. (7)

1803 Dated Specimen

A shortened specimen with an 1803 dated lockplate is in the Fuller Collection (see page 16). It bears serial number 2218, and the marks on the top of the barrel correspond with those on the Model 1806 Pistols. "C.P. 944" is stamped to the rear of the barrel marks, and "P" together with an underscored inverted "v" is stamped 4 in. from the breech. The stock measures 8 1/2 in. from the butt to the comb, and "C. P. 944" is stamped on the left hand side of the stock opposite the lock. The rear band is 11 1/8 in. from the end of the breech, and is 7/8 in. wide at the top, and 1 11/16 in. wide at the bottom. The band spring is 2 5/8 in. long. The trigger guard is 11 1/2 in. long, and the trigger guard straps have long pointed ends. The butt plate is stamped with serial number 2218.

This serial number 2218, and the other serial numbers mentioned above may indicate that the Bomford production records are incomplete, and that a fairly large number of muskets were made at Harpers Ferry prior to 1801.

Model 1795 Musketoon (?)

A dealer's catalogue lists a "Musketoon", 1803 dated lockplate. (8)

And one authority reports Harpers Ferry "Model 1795" Muskets with barrels that measure only 42 in. ("3 inches shorter than the common size"), expressing the opinion that these arms were probably made for Naval use. (8a)

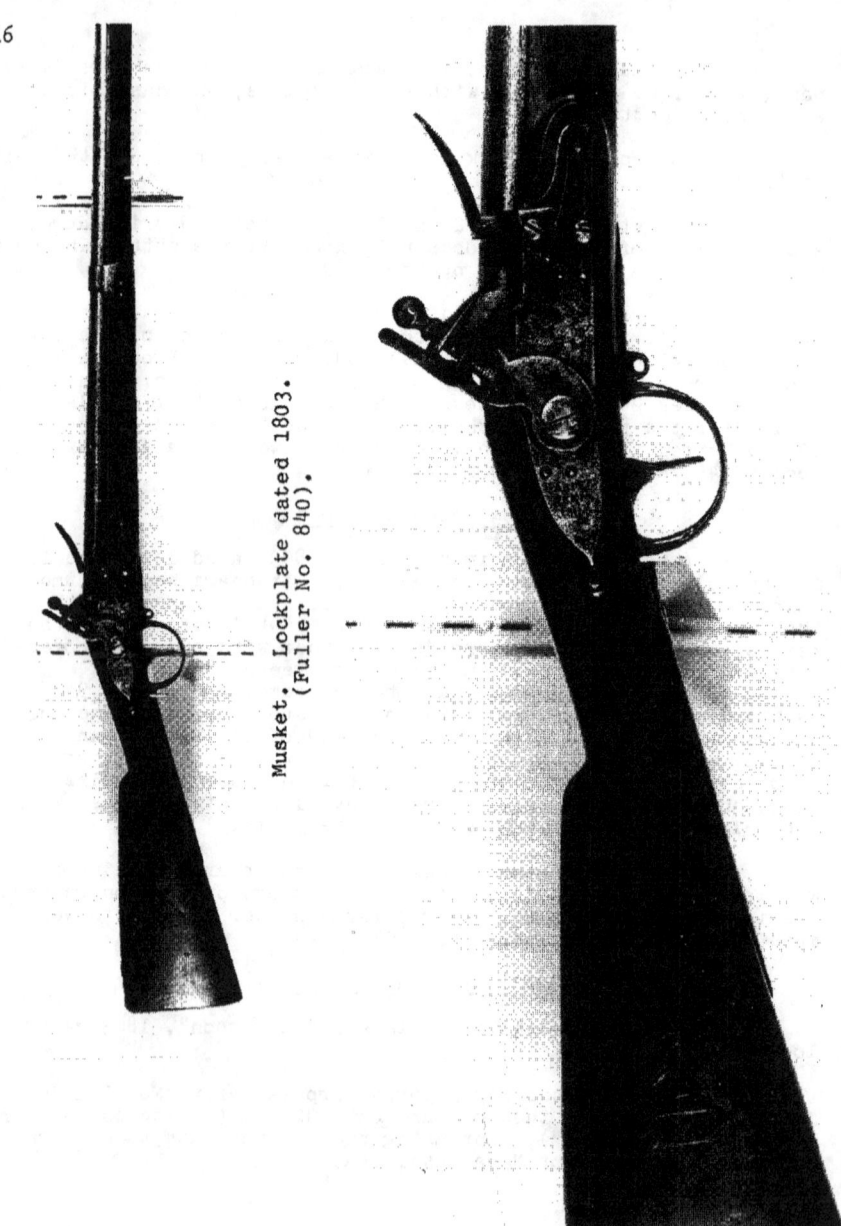

Musket. Lockplate dated 1803. (Fuller No. 840).

Musket. Lockplate dated 1803. Note curl in tail of frizzen. (Lehmann).

Apparently, the musket with the 1800 dated lockplate described by Patterson, the Robertson musket, and the Fuller musket (except for the shortened barrel) are typical of the Harpers Ferry Model 1795's, and apparently, Harpers Ferry regularly produced muskets of this same Model, with several non-Model-changing variations, up until 1816.

"Model 1808"

Many persons classify some of the earliest muskets made at the two national armories as Model 1808's, and this unofficial classification may or may not be correct as regards muskets produced at Springfield. However, there does not appear to be any such thing as a Harpers Ferry Model 1808.

The Springfield Model 1808's seem to be the same or virtually the same as the muskets that Harpers Ferry had been producing since 1800, and continued to produce until 1816.

In 1808, a notable year for both of the national armories, the Federal Government undertook to provide arms "either by purchase or by manufacture" for the militia of the several states or territories (and thereafter, until 1840, annual quotas of arms were distributed "in proportion to the number of effective militia in each state and territory"). In 1808, Harpers Ferry made 3,051 muskets as opposed to only 50 made in 1807, and as opposed to a total of only 297 made in 1804 through 1806. And in 1808, or thereabouts, several private manufacturers contracted to produce "musquets with bayonet, Charleville pattern", the probabilities being that at least some of the private contractors were furnished patterns made at Harpers Ferry.

In a letter dated December 9, 1808, Tench Coxe, the Purveyor of Supplies, writes of "arms received through the War Department" from Harpers Ferry, and that "two stands have been retained as patterns, and the others have been delivered to the contractors, to aid them in keeping their workmen to uniformity and goodness of workmanship, as well as in the fitting and joining of the parts, as in the form and finish of these parts respectively". (9)

However, the patterns made by Harpers Ferry in 1808 were probably duplicates or nearly duplicates of the muskets that Harpers Ferry had been producing since 1800.

Between 1800 and 1808, there were, of course, some variations. Between the beginning of 1808, and the end of 1811, Harpers Ferry commenced using a new eagle-US lockplate marking, and somewhere along the line, round end trigger guard straps replaced those with long pointed ends. Also, the lockplates

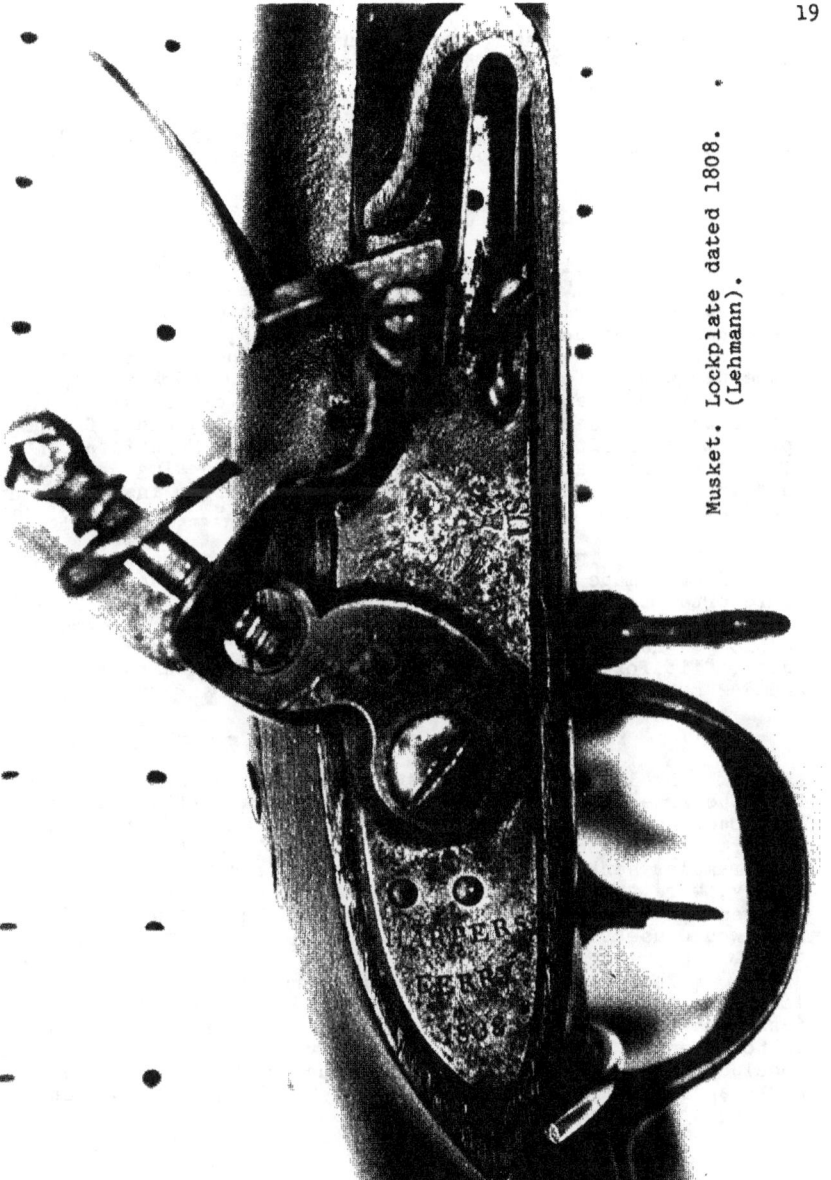

Musket. Lockplate dated 1808. (Lehmann).

dated 1808, et seq., are more bulbous in the rear, and according to Satterlee, the "Model 1808" has a lockplate that is 1/4 in. longer than the 6 1/4 in. lockplate of the Model 1795. (10)

But, all in all, the changes made between 1800 and 1808 in Harpers Ferry muskets are not sufficient in scope to constitute a change in Model.

Apparently, in 1809, the quality of United States muskets was subjected to a close scrutiny, and one conclusion was that "even the Harpers Ferry muskets cannot stand a rigid inspection". Harpers Ferry musket, No. 2089, was tested and found defective - - - "the ramrod, bayonet and lock of the sample inspected were defective either in material or workmanship" - - - and by letter dated July 15, 1809, Secretary of War William Eustis wrote to James Stubblefield, a Virginian, and a Colonel (probably of militia), who had been serving as Superintendent of Harpers Ferry since the Spring of 1807, directing Stubblefield to "make it your duty to establish the most rigid inspection and proof of all arms hereafter manufactured at" Harpers Ferry. (11)

Early in 1810, Lieutenant Colonel John Whiting of the 4th Infantry made an inspection at Harpers Ferry, and in March, he reported to Eustis that the guns made there were "of superior workmanship", and that "the rifles and pistols are of excellent fashion". As of January 1, 1810, there were on hand at Harpers Ferry, "fit for service", 12,873 muskets "marked Harpers Ferry", and 342 muskets "stocked and mounted at Harpers Ferry". (12)

By letter dated August 1, 1811, Coxe advised Eustis that the Arsenal (apparently that on the Schuylkill) had received "proposed new pattern muskets * * * of the Harpers Ferry manufacture of A.D. 1811 * * * numbered 24, 187 to 24, 211, but not of a regular series". The muskets, which apparently varied widely, were then gone over, and the best nine were picked out and removed to Coxe's office, Coxe's idea being that the "workmen" would use them "as future guides in thier armories". (13)

Patterson notes a Harpers Ferry musket, 1816 dated lockplate, with a 45 in. barrel, pointed trigger guard straps, flat face and bevel edge lockplate, and a horizontal, round bottom, fenced iron pan cast integrally with the lockplate. He concludes that it is the same or virtually the same as the Harpers Ferry specimen with the 1800 dated lockplate except, of course, for the lockplate markings. (14)

However, another, and probably later Harpers Ferry musket with an 1816 dated lockplate (Ahalt Specimen, see below) differs.

Russell, considering the product of both national armories, concludes that the Model 1795, in its various "issues" is consistent in having three bands, in being approximately Caliber .69, and in having a barrel length ranging from 42 in. to 44 3/4 in., a stock length ranging from 54 1/4 in. to 56 1/2 in., an overall length ranging from 57 in. to 59 3/5 in., a trigger guard ranging in length from 10 1/4 in. to 13 in. with strap ends varying from pointed to round, and a rear sling swivel affixed to a stud located in front of the trigger guard. (15)

But, in applying Russell's standards to Harpers Ferry muskets, one must note exceptions such as the musket, 1816 dated lockplate, with a 45 in. barrel reported by Patterson; a specimen, 1814 dated lockplate, with a 45 in. barrel listed in a dealer's catalogue (16); and Satterlee's statement that the "Model 1808's" are 60 1/2 in. long overall, and have a 45 1/2 in. barrel. (17)

Model 1812

In a letter dated November 11, 1811, and addressed to Eustis, Coxe expressed the opinion that "a standard rifle, a standard musket, and a standard pistol appear to be the most desirable objects". (18)

Then, on June 18, 1812, the Congress declared war on England, and this declaration, if not the disturbed conditions that preceded it, stimulated a reappraisal of United States firearms. In one step directed towards standarization, Callender Irvine, Commissary General of Purchases, "procured a French manufactured musket, having all the latest improvements", and then "consulted practical ingenious men in whose integrity (he) could confide, and requested them to point out such alterations from the French musket as they might deem of any importance". Next, Irvine "caused a musket to be constructed under the direction of" Marine T. Wickham, "a superior artist, * * * who had been employed for many years as master armorer at Harpers Ferry". (19) And in 1812, Peter Pelaux, working under Wickham at the United States Armory on the Schuylkill in Philadelphia, completed the musket.

Irvine described Pelaux as "a very complete workman" - - - "a very superior workman", and described the Wickham-Pelaux musket as "superior to any hitherto constructed, in any part of the world." The Wickham-Pelaux musket, according to Irvine, combined "the latest improvements" (in muskets manufactured by the United States and by France), its "only important deviation from the French musket being "in the securing of the bayonet".

Musket lockplate dated 1813.
(Karr).

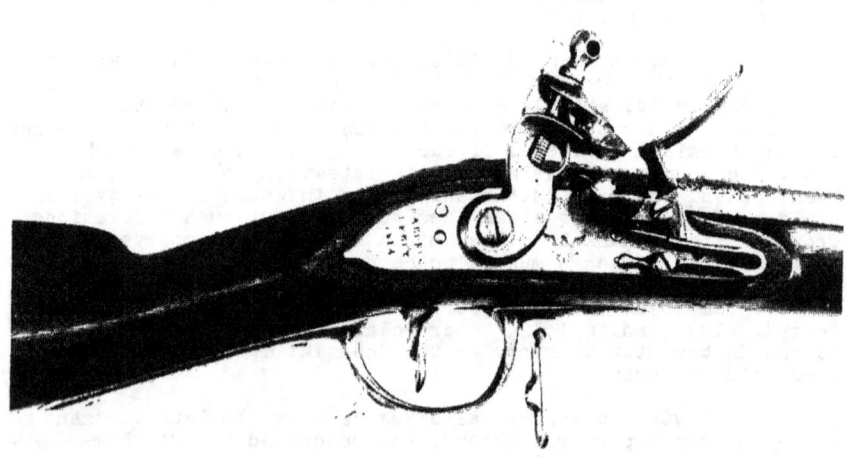

Musket. Lockplate dated 1814.
(Fuller No. 837).

The bayonet on the Wickham-Pelaux musket was affixed by means of a set screw, and could be removed only by using a screwdriver, but when general issue muskets were produced, they were equipped with socket type bayonets. (20)

By letter dated December 2, 1812, Irvine directed Wickham to proceed to Washington and present the musket to Eustis. And if Eustis approved the musket, Wickham was then to proceed to Harpers Ferry, and there "superintend the making of 15 or 20" muskets". (21)

Eustis approved the musket as did "all the officers of Govt. resident at Washington, one only excepted". (22)

By letter dated December 8, 1812, Eustis ordered Stubblefield, the Superintendent at Harpers Ferry, to make "without delay" twenty-four muskets "conformable to" the Wickham-Pelaux musket "which will be delivered to you by the bearer, Mr. Wickham" and Eustis further directed that the Wickham-Pelaux musket be the model "on which the muskets will be manufactured at the Public Armory after working up the parts which have already been prepared on the old model". (23)

However, the exigencies of the war probably caused a change in plans - - - in a letter dated November 30, 1813, Irvine indicates that Harpers Ferry was ordered to make only six muskets "corresponding * * * in every respect" with the Wickham-Pelaux musket, and the Bomford production records show that in 1813, only five pattern muskets were produced. (24)

Moreover, the exigencies of war were not conducive to any changes in design - - - muskets of any sort were sorely needed - - - and whatever Departmental calm may have existed must have been disturbed when, in 1814, the British captured Washington, and burned the White House.

The war ended in January of 1815 with the battle of New Orleans, and Harpers Ferry in 1816, but not prior to 1816, began to produce what 20th Century collectors call Model 1812's.

One main change in the Model 1812 was the shortening of the barrel from the 44-45 in. range to the 42 in., and a 42 in. barrel specimen with an 1816 dated lockplate is in the collection of Charles Ahalt.

The Ahalt specimen has a lockplate measuring 6 3/8 in. by 1 1/4 in., and a 10 in. trigger guard that has straps with round ends. The stock measures 52 3/4 in., and has a small comb. The lockplate has a flat face, the iron pan is cast integrally with the lockplate, and the cock has a part round, part flat face. The band springs are forward of the two rear bands, and the rear

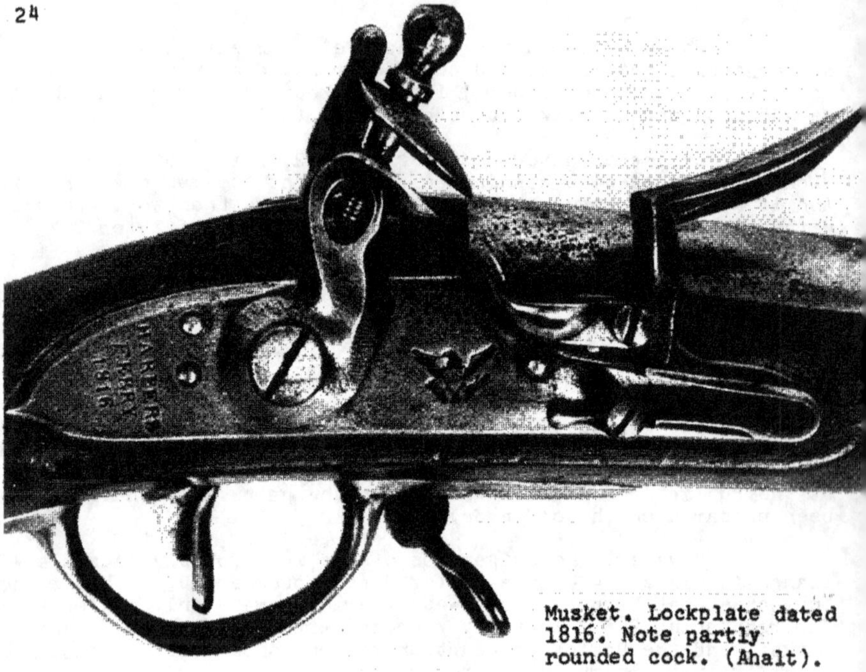

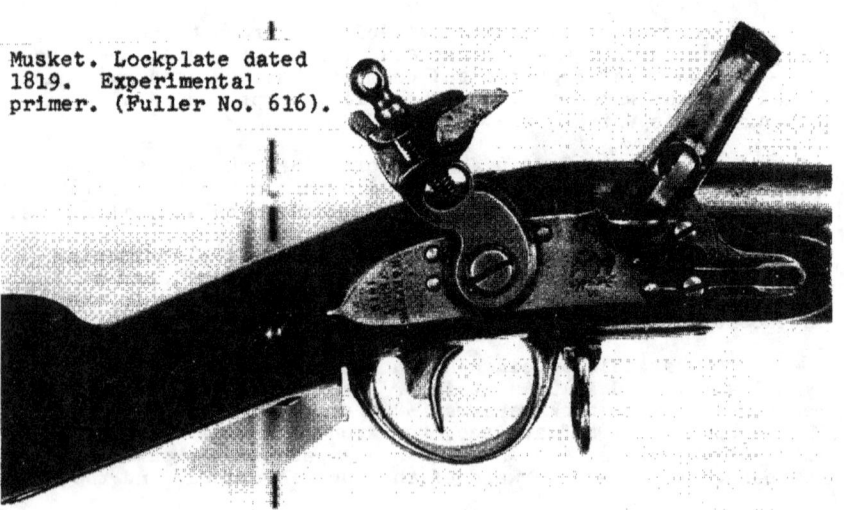

Musket. Lockplate dated 1816. Note partly rounded cock. (Ahalt).

Musket. Lockplate dated 1819. Experimental primer. (Fuller No. 616).

band is 11 1/4 in. from the breech, and is 3/4 in. wide at the top, and 1 1/4 in. wide at the bottom. The middle band is 23 3/8 in. from the breech, and is 7/8 in. wide at both the top and the bottom. The rear band spring measures 2 1/8 in., and both the middle band spring and the front band spring measure 2 3/16 in. The breech tang is 2 1/4 in. long. There is no "US" on the butt plate. The barrel markings correspond with those on the Model 1806 Pistols. The left side of the stock is stamped (script) with a "V" over "JS", and a "V", and a "AT". There is a brass blade sight on the rear strap of the front band.

There is a specimen, 1818 dated lockplate, in the Fuller Collection that is equipped with an experimental primer which must have been designed by a person who had no fear of premature blindness. The primer's power magazine takes the place of the frizzen, and one-half turn of the hand screw located at the top of the magazine allows enough powder for one priming to flow into the pan.

The band springs on the Fuller specimen are forward of the two rear bands, and the rear band spring is 2 1/2 in. long. The barrel is marked with an eagle head and an "M" (for model, i.e., pattern). The cock has a flat face, but according to Satterlee, most of the Model 1812's have round face cocks. (25)

Neither the Ahalt specimen nor the Fuller specimen has a cheek recess on the left side of the stock as do the Springfield Model 1812's, and apparently, none of the Harpers Ferry Model 1812's have cheek recesses.

Model 1812 (Artillery)

Gluckman reports a Harpers Ferry specimen, 1817 dated lockplate, with an integrally cast pan, and having an overall length of 51 3/4 in., a stock measuring 48 3/8 in., a 36 in. barrel marked "US" in an oval, and an eagle head "P" in an oval, and with bands spaced (from front to rear) the following distances from the muzzle 3 1/8 in., 9 1/4 in., and 9 1/8 in. The stock has a comb. (26)

Notes

(1) Collection of Ralph A. Frederick. Letter Gun Report Vol. V, No. 12 (May 1960) p. 4.
(2) Kimball Catalogue 9, Item K54.
(3) Fuller, Whitney Firearms 96.
(4) Sawyer MSS Notes
(5) Patterson 23.
(6) Kimball Catalogue 9, Item HFIX.
(7) Letter Gun Report, Vol. III, No. 6 (November 1957) p.4.
(8) Kimball Catalogue 4, Item M18A.

(8a) Mitchell, "United States Musket Model 1795" p. 123.
(9) Fuller, Whitney Firearms 90.
(10) Satterlee 275.
(11) Hicks (II) 26.
(12) Ibid. 132-4.
(13) Ibid. 34.
(14) Patterson 23.
(15) Russell 155.
(16) Jackson Catalogue 24, Item 309A.
(17) Satterlee 169.
(18) Hicks II 36.
(19) Hicks 43.
(20) Ibid. 40-41.
(21) Ibid. 40.
(22) Ibid. 43-4.
(23) Ibid. 39.
(24) Ibid. 44.
(25) Satterlee 275.
(26) Gluckman 144.

Bank note dated 1815.
Note curl in tail of
frizzen. (Affleck).

27

Rifleman with Model 1803
Rifle. 1st Rifle Regiment.
Winter Uniform. 1812-1815.

II. THE EARLY RIFLES

During the American Revolution, the rifle proved its worth.

A musket could, of course, be fired more rapidly - - - the seating of a musket ball required little more than a wad and a firm jab with the ramrod, whereas a rifle ball had to be wrapped in a greasy cloth or leather patch, and then literally pounded through the barrel from the muzzle to the powder in the breech. Moreover, the early rifles were not equipped with bayonets, and left the slow-reloading riflemen vulnerable to bayonet charges.

However, a ball fired from a musket tends to wobble and arbitrarily choose its own path of flight, much as does the baseball's pitcher's "slow ball", whereas a spinning ball fired from a rifle travels within reason to the spot at which it is aimed. This greater accuracy more than offset, in some military situations, the rifle's slow-firing and bayonet-less shortcomings, and when riflemen complemented musketmen or vice versa, both were more effective.

In 1799, the Congress authorized the formation of a rifle regiment.

Model 1800 (?)

Sawyer labels the earliest Harpers Ferry rifles Model 1800's, but offers no explanation. He states that the earliest known specimen, in the Pugsley Collection, has a lockplate dated 1803. (1)

Van Renssalear states that the earliest known Harpers Ferry rifle has an 1801 dated lockplate. (2)

The writer of this study does not know why Sawyer used the "Model 1800" label, and he does not know anything about Van Renssalear's 1801 Harpers Ferry rifle.

A Model 1803 Rifle, 1803 dated lockplate, with serial number 844, and another with serial number 500-odd on the bottom of the barrel (3) may be indications that Harpers Ferry made rifles prior to 1803.

Full Octagonal Barrels and Full Maple Stocks (?)

Gluckman reports Model 1803's with full octagonal barrels (4), but he does not elaborate. And there is a rumor of the existence of an early Harpers Ferry rifle with a full maple stock.

Patterson advises that he once owned an octagonal barrel rifle with a Harpers Ferry lockplate dated 1841 (converted from flintlock to percussion), and expresses the opinion that only the lockplate was made at Harpers Ferry. (5) The writer of this study has examined another, similar rifle that was merely a "Kentucky" with a Harpers Ferry lockplate, and apparently, none of the parts other than the lockplate (and perhaps the remainder of the lock) were made at Harpers Ferry.

Model 1803

In May of 1803, Secretary of War Henry Dearborn wrote to Joseph Perkin, the Superintendent at Harpers Ferry, stating not only that there was "a deficiency of rifles in the public arsenals", but also that the rifles on hand were not "as well calculated for actual service as could be wished". Dearborn also stated that it was "considered advisable to have a suitable number of judicially constructed rifles manufactured at the (Harpers Ferry) Armory" under Perkin's direction, and directed that the "necessary measures for commencing the manufacture" of the rifles be taken "as soon as may be after completing the muskets now in hand".

As regards design, the arms to which both military and civilian riflemen had become accustomed were the American "long rifles", now called "Kentuckies". However, Dearborn had "such convincing proof of the advantage of short rifles * * * over the long ones (commonly used) in actual service as to leave no doubt in (his) mind of preferring the short rifle, with larger calibers than the long ones", and of preferring "stiff steel ramrods instead of wooden ones".

"The great facility which such rifles afford in charging", Dearborn noted, "in addition to their being less liable to become fouled by firing, gives a decided advantage to men of equal skill and dexterity over those armed with the common long rifle".

Accordingly, Dearborn specified that the barrels of the new rifles not exceed 33 in. in length, that they be round from the muzzle to within 10 in. of the breech, that they be bored for a 1/2 oz. ball (Caliber .54), and that they not be "of an unnecessary thickness especially in the round part". (6)

Lewis and Clark Rifles

Meanwhile, Thomas Jefferson, convinced that the United States was destined to expand westward, dreamed of Americans crossing the Rocky Mountains, and travelling down the legendary Great River of the West to the Pacific Ocean. In 1801, he became President, and in March of that year, he appointed, as his personal secretary, Meriwether Lewis, a twenty-six year old Captain of the 1st Infantry who had just completed six years service on the frontier, and whom Jefferson later described as "brave, prudent, habituated to the woods and familiar with Indian manners and character".

Then, on January 18, 1803, Jefferson laid a secret message before the Congress proposing a semi-surreptitious exploration of the unknown sources of the Missouri River, and ways thence westward to the Pacific, passing through country that was then, for the most part, under the flag of France, and under the provincial administration of Spain. Congress gave its approval, Jefferson named Lewis to head the Expedition, and much of the Expedition's equipment was made at or procured from Harpers Ferry - - - on April 20, 1803, Lewis wrote to Jefferson, from Lancaster, Pennsylvania, that "my rifles, tomahawks & knives are preparing at Harpers Ferry, and are already in the state of readiness that leaves me little doubt of their being in readiness in due time".

Lewis' list of requirements included fifteen "rifles", twenty-four pipe tomahawks, thirty-six pipe tomahawks "for Indian presents", twenty-four large knives, fifteen "powder horns and pouches complete", fifteen pairs of "bullet molds", fifteen "wipers or gun worms", fifteen "ball screws", fifteen "gun slings", "extra parts of locks and tools for replacing arms", and forty "fish giggs such as the Indians use with a single barb point". (7) All of these items were probably made at Harpers Ferry, and Harpers Ferry also made a collapsible iron frame for a canoe - - - Lewis stated (in his letter to Jefferson of April 20, 1803) that "My detention at Harpers Ferry was unavoidable for one month, a period much greater than could reasonably have been calculated on; my greatest difficulty was the frame of the canoe, which could not be completed without my personal attention to such portion of it as would enable the workmen to understand the design perfectly" - - - and at Harpers Ferry, Lewis also procured a small grindstone.

On July 8th, Lewis wrote to Jefferson, this time from Harpers Ferry, stating that "yesterday I shot my guns and examined the several articles which have been manufactered for me at this place", and advising that the equipment was ready, and that, via wagon, it "will go on early in the morning". And on July 22, 1803, Lewis reported to Jefferson that a "wagon from Harpers

Ferry arrived today, bringing everything with which she (Harpers Ferry) was charged in good order".

Of course, there is a possibility that the rifles which Lewis obtained from Harpers Ferry were not made at Harpers Ferry.

Some authorities assert that Lewis designed the Model 1803 Rifle, and he did possess frontier and military experience, and he may have been infected with some of his sponsor's (Jefferson's) inventive genius, but there is no proof that Lewis designed the Model 1803 Rifles.

Moreover, it has not even been proven that the Expedition's fifteen rifles were Model 1803's.

In July of 1803, when Lewis received his rifles from Harpers Ferry, the Model 1803 was apparently still in the model stage - - - it was not until December 2, 1803, that Dearborn wrote to Perkin approving the "ironed ribed" rifle that had been manufactured at Harpers Ferry under Perkin's direction. Dearborn, expressing the opinion that the pattern was "excellent", asked only that "the upper end of the upper thimble should be a little bell muzzled to receive the introduction of the ramrod more conveniently", that the "cut in the sight near the breech should be a little wider", and that "a brass ferrule (be) placed at the end of the stock near the tail pipe, to prevent that part of the stock from splitting". (8)

Moreover, Lewis' order for fifteen "gun slings" indicates that the Expedition's fifteen rifles had full stocks - - - it would be difficult to attach a sling to a Model 1803 or to any other half stock rifle.

Of course, a half stock rifle with a short barrel would be advantageous to a horseman - - - a short, half stock rifle carries well in a scabbard - - - but Lewis planned to travel mostly by boat, and the Expedition actually did very little of its travelling on horseback.

The Expedition did not set forth until 1804, and some Model 1803 Rifles may well have joined the Expedition prior to the date of its departure.

On Sunday, April 6, 1804, William Clark, the Expedition's co-leader, recorded that "several of the countrey people" were in "camp shooting with" the members of the Expedition, and that "all" of the "countrey" people "git beet and lose their money", and on April 10, Clark ordered that "every man have 100 balls for their rifles & 2 lbs. of buckshot for those with musquets, etc.". (9)

Lewis' reports include an entry that on one occasion, when "the guns of Drewyer (Drouillard) and Sergeant Pryor were out of order, the first was fitted with a new lock, and the broken tumbler of the latter was replaced by a duplicate, which had been made at Harpers Ferry, where the gun itself had been manufactured. But for our precaution in bringing extra locks, and duplicate parts of the locks, most of our guns would be now useless, in spite of the skill and ingenuity of John Shields in repairing them. Fortunately, as it is, we are able to record here that they are all in good order". (10)

Out west, also, the Expedition had trouble in bringing down the grizzly, and this possibly is an indication that the Expedition's rifles were of small caliber (as opposed to the Model 1803's large caliber).

In this connection, it is interesting to note the similar experiences of a slightly later expedition headed by Zebulon Montgomery Pike, a First Lieutenant of the 1st Infantry. On June 24, 1805, without President Jefferson's prior knowledge, Pike was ordered to explore the Mississippi River to its northern-most source, and later, while up the Mississippi, Pike complained that his rifle balls were too small for bringing down a buffalo. "The Ball should not be more than 30 to the pound; or an Ounce Ball would still be preferable", wrote Pike, indicating that his rifles were not Model 1803's.

On April 30, 1806, Pike returned to St. Louis, but on July 15, 1806, he departed as head of an expedition ordered to explore the upper Arkansas River and the southwest portions of the Louisiana Purchase. On this 1806-7 expedition, Pike's men had no trouble killing buffalo, and this possibly is an indication that the 1806-7 expedition carried Model 1803's. (11)

In 1807, Lewis, triumphantly touring the east, posed in buckskins for the painting of his portrait, and the rifle held by him had a full stock, sling swivels, and a checkered grip of the sort sometimes found on "officer's models". (12)

The Model 1803 was purely a military arm, and it seems logical that Lewis or any other explorer would have chosen a more accurate long barrel rifle of the Kentucky type. Furthermore, the indications are that Lewis' fifteen rifles probably had full stocks and sling swivels, and since the expedition was ostensibly peaceful and scientific, the possibilities are that Lewis' fifteen rifles did not have the usual military (armory) markings.

When the Expedition returned to St. Louis, "Sundry Rifles, Muskets * * * & other public property remaining on hand at the termination of the Expedition * * * were disposed of at Public Auction". (13)

Cover Illustration

The Lewis and Clark Expedition included among its members the interpreter Toussaint Charbonneau, the young Shoshone Indian girl Sacagawea, and their baby. Charbonneau, lazy and inept, was almost as worthless to the Expedition as was the infant, but Sacagawea was of great assistance. Raised by the Hidatsa Indians who had stolen her from the Shoshone, she knew at least two Indian dialects, and a good deal of local geography.

Sacagawea's greatest worth was proven when the Expedition, having arrived at the headwaters of the Missouri, needed horses to carry it across the Rocky Mountains to the navigable head waters of the Columbia. At this critical juncture, on August 17, 1805, the Expedition encountered, and Sacagawea was recognized by Shoshone, and because of Sacagawea, the Expedition was able to obtain horses from the Shoshone.

The painting by Charles M. Russell (1864-1926) America's great "cowboy" artist, depicts Lewis, rifle in hand, watching Sacagawea's reunion with her people.

Much of Russell's work has been criticized on the grounds that his cattle, his horses, and his humans are idealized - - - one cowboy complained that Russell painted only "pure breds" - - - but most of the people that Russell painted, including Lewis and Sacagawea were, subjectively, "pure breds".

The high quality of Russell's backgrounds can be fully appreciated only by those who have viewed the magnificent western plains and mountains.

*The cover illustration, in its original form, is full-color. Clearfield has reproduced it here in black and white.

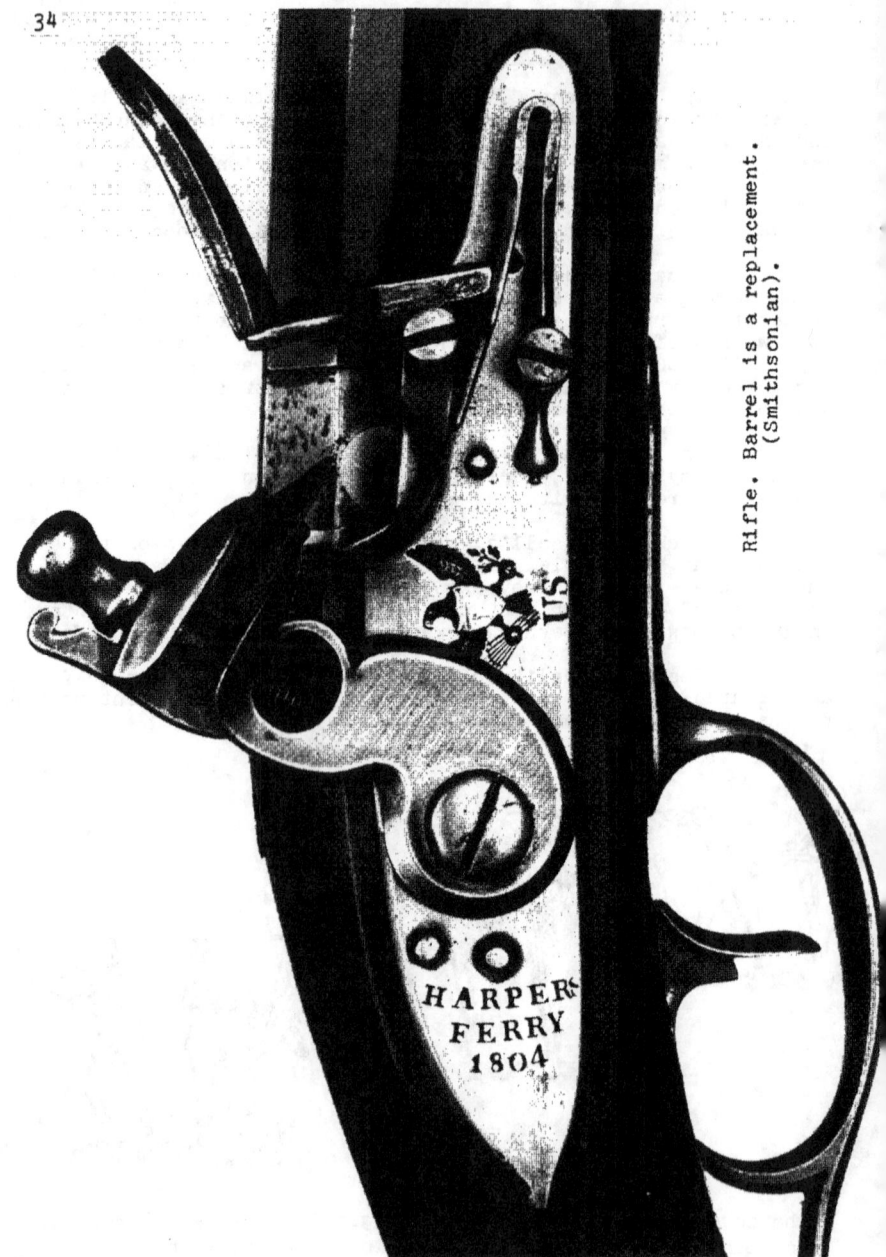

Rifle. Barrel is a replacement. (Smithsonian).

Model 1803 (continued)

On November 1, 1804, Dearborn wrote to Perkin, noting that Perkin's "hands", i.e., the workmen at Harpers Ferry, have now acquired sufficient knowledge in manufacturing of rifles", and stating that it was "advisable to continue making them until 4000 shall be completed". (14)

The 4000 order was completed in 1807.

The specimen, 1803 dated lockplate, with serial number 844, and the other with serial number 500-odd on the bottom of the barrel may be indications that a large number of rifles (Model 1803's or rifles of an earlier Model) were made at Harpers Ferry in 1803.

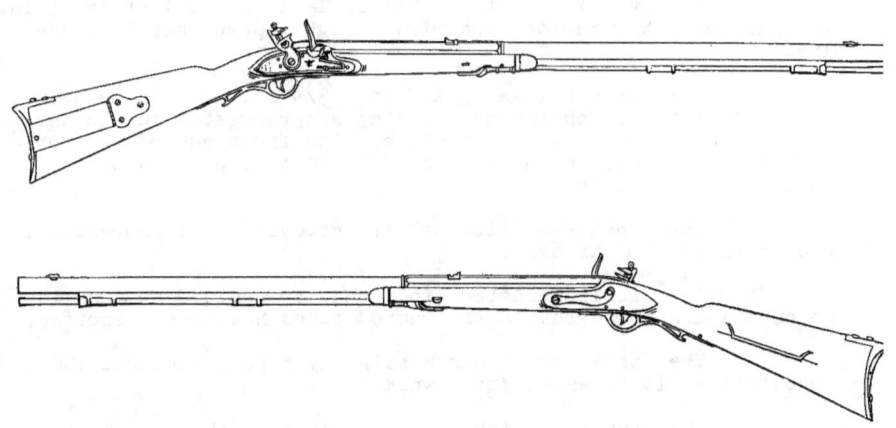

The collection of William M. Locke also includes a specimen, 1804 dated lockplate, with serial number 974; a specimen, 1805 dated lockplate, with serial number 1895; and a specimen, 1806 dated lockplate, with serial number 3207.

1803-4-5-6 Dated Specimens

The lockplate is 5 1/4 in. by 1 in., and the iron pan is forged integrally with the lockplate. (14a)

The stock is approximately 26 in. long, and has a comb that measures about 1/2 in. The stock measures approximately 11 in. from the comb to the heel of the butt. The stock is fastened by a single sliding key.

The barrel is approximately 33 in. long - - - at least one 32 in. barrel is reported - - - and the barrel is half octagonal and half round, with the octagonal rear portion of the barrel being approximately 11 in. long. The boring and the grooving vary - - - Sawyer states that for many years the arm was in the experimental stage, and that "no two have lands and grooves exactly alike" - - - Sawyer reports one specimen as having "an heptagonal instead of a circular bore". (15)

The barrel markings are the same as those on the Model 1806 Pistol.

The overall length of the rifle is approximately 48 in., and including the ramrod, the rifle weighs approximately 9 1/4 lbs.

The brass trigger guard is 5 3/4 in. long. The brass patch box cover is opened by pressing a spring stud set in the tang on top of the brass butt plate. The front end of the forearm is strengthened by a brass band. The tail pipe is brass, as is the side plate.

The rib has a "fluting" or "groove" on its underside, and is welded to the barrel.

The two iron ramrod pipes that are welded to the rib measure 1 1/2 in. each. Brass ramrod pipes have been reported.

The steel ramrod has a slightly cupped end, and the opposite end is threaded for a wormer.

The open rear sight, that is mounted about 8 in. from the breech, and the brass blade front sight are set for a range of 50 yards.

The iron pipes, the barrel, and the rib are all acid browned.

- - - - - - - - - - - - - - - - - - - -

On November 11, 1811, Tench Coxe, the Purveyor of Supplies, wrote a letter to Secretary of War William Eustis criticizing the Model 1803. The "costly and heavy rib", wrote Coxe, "appears to serve no other purpose than to secure these two rod pipes to the barrel or to the combined frame", and it appeared to Coxe to be "worth considering" that a rib of 2 or 2 1/2 in. would be enough for the upper (front) ramrod pipe, that there be a cast brass cap or at least a "stoght" cap of sheet brass, and that there be a "good black walnut stock", i.e., a full stock (and Coxe suggested that walnut was "perhaps better than maple").

Secondly, he stated that he was "assured that the iron head of the ramrod will destroy the rifling", and suggested that the first two inches of the ramrod be brass or that the ramrod be wood - - - "wooden rods are common to rifles".

Thirdly, he classified the 33 in. barrel as "so short as to be dangerous", but suggested that the rifles would be safe if the barrels were 38 in. long.

Coxe also expressed "doubt that the insertion" of the front brass sight "endangers the barrel"; he felt that the lockplate (of both the rifle and the pistol) was too small "to give room for the works"; and he was of the opinion that the brass side plate (of both the pistol and the rifle) would "soon wear in the female screw thread".

Finally noting that "the butt-box for the wiper, flint and rag, is made to open by a pin near the bottom of the back of the butt, where it is liable to be struck by stone and stumps, and opened", Coxe thought it better to have the opening pin located on the side of the butt. (16)

On January 1, 1810, there were on hand at Harpers Ferry, "fit for service", 3113 "short" rifles "marked Harpers Ferry", and 188 "long" rifles. (17)

In 1813, plans were laid to form three additional rifle regiments, and in that year, Harpers Ferry produced four pattern rifles probably for use by private contractors.

In the Spring of 1814, General John Armstrong, the Secretary of War, ordered Harpers Ferry to produce 3000 rifles. By June 1st, Harpers Ferry had completed two specimens, and by the end of September, 100 rifles were on hand, with eight to ten more being completed each day. (18) But the urgency was greater, and in October of 1814, James Monroe, then Secretary of War, ordered Harpers Ferry to send to Springfield a pattern rifle and three Harpers Ferry workmen "well acquainted with the construction of rifles". And on the same day, the Superintendent at Springfield was ordered "without delay" to "make such arrangements as will eventually enable you to manufacture 500 rifles per month". (19)

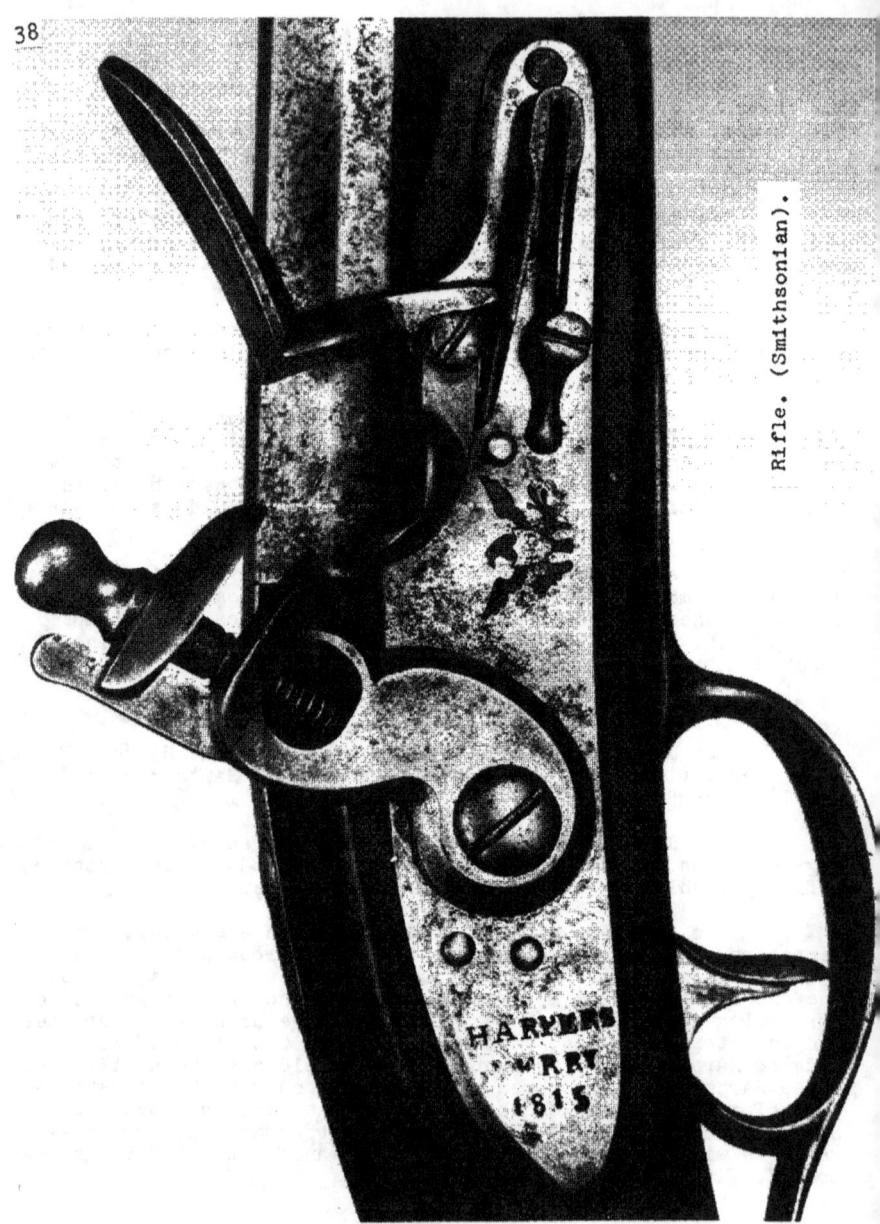

38 Rifle. (Smithsonian).

However, making rifles was quite different from making muskets, and Springfield's rifle producing efforts bogged down. Although Springfield completed some 3000 rifle locks, ribs, "box springs", slides, barrel slides, back sights and wipers by June of 1816, Springfield then had no rifle stocks, and Lt. Col. Roswell Lee, the Springfield Superintendent, pointed out the fact that even if stocks were made available, it would "take them a long time to season". But Lee reported that the rifle parts on hand at Springfield were "good and of the same pattern as those of the Ferry", and after checking with James Stubblefield, the Superintendent at Harpers Ferry, Lee suggested that the parts be shipped to Harpers Ferry where "they are making rifles and have everything in readiness".

Lee renewed this suggestion in a letter dated February 13, 1817, and in a postscript, he stated: "As we have only about 300 barrels welded for the rifles, they might be made conformable to the model with the bands (the ribs in that case would remain on hand) * * * ". (20)

In referring to "the model with the bands", Lee was, without doubt, referring to the Model 1817 Rifle.

In August of 1817, the Springfield parts were shipped to Harpers Ferry, and in September of 1819, in "part payment" for the parts, Harpers Ferry shipped 250 completed rifles to Greenleaf's Point, the Washington, D. C., Arsenal (21), where they were to be credited to Springfield. It seems reasonable to conclude that the parts manufactured by Springfield were for 36 in. barrel rifles.

Patterson states that Harpers Ferry made 33 in. barrel (or approximately 33 in. barrel) specimens in 1814 through 1816, and states that he is skeptical of 36 in. barrel specimens with 1814 and 1815 dated lockplates. (22) However, Colonel Lewis reports a 36 in. barrel specimen with an 1815 dated lockplate. (23)

The 33 in. barrel rifles had a tremendous recoil, and the lengthening of the barrel may have lessened the "kick".

<u>Specimens Dated 1814, et seq.</u>

These rifles differ in some respects from those with lockplates dated 1803-6.

Their eagle-U.S. lockplate markings are different.

On specimens with lockplates dated 1814, et seq., that have 33 in. (or approximately 33 in.) barrels, the overall length is approximately 49 in., and the stock is approximately 29 in. long.

There are reports of barrels as long as 33 7/8 in.

On specimens that have 36 in. (or approximately 36 in.) barrels, the overall length is approximately 52 in., the stock is approximately 30 in. long, and the octagonal portion of the barrel is approximately 13 in. long. In general, these and some of the other parts are proportioned according to the length of the barrel.

The brass trigger guard is approximately 8 in. long - - - a 7 1/2 in. trigger guard has been reported. And some of the later specimens have the cup end ramrod with a brass tip that is standard on rifles of the next Model (Model 1817).

- - - - - - - - - - - - - - - - - - -

Model 1803 Rifles were used against the Indians, in the War of 1812, and to a lesser degree, in the Mexican War. They were also used to some extent by the Navy against West Indian pirates and Barbary pirates. (24) They were used by the rifle regiments, by the 26th Infantry, and by a number of militia units during the War of 1812. (25)

"Officer's Models"

Sawyer states that "as the officers of a rifle regiment carried rifles instead of swords, the government provided them with weapons slightly lighter in weight and somewhat more ornamental in respect to engraving, checkering and the shape of the small parts than the arms of the enlisted men". (26)

A dealer's catalogue lists a specimen, 1804 dated lockplate, that was altered in Perth, Scotland, by the substitution of a patent breech with a platinum vent, by putting a horn tip in the foreend, and by checkering the small of the stock. (27)

The specimen, 1806 dated lockplate, in the Locke collection has an engraved patch box, as does the Smithsonian specimen, 1815 dated lockplate. See page 155.

Set Triggers

Sawyer reports that some of the rifles were equipped with set triggers, and states of this feature and others that "these details evidently belong in the 'made-to-order' class, and were individualities granted the request or demands of certain noted marksmen who enlisted; for in those days a noted rifleman was a little king who honored the service by enlisting in it". (28)

Notes

(1) Sawyer 131.
(2) Van Rensselear 111.
(3) Serial number 844 is in the collection of William M. Locke. Serial number 500-odd reported by John Stapleton.
(4) Gluckman 183.
(5) Letter C. Meade Patterson to author. January 28, 1968.
(6) Hicks 25.
(7) Jackson, Letters of the Lewis and Clark Expedition 70 and 72-73.
(8) Hicks 25.
(9) Clark, Field Notes of Captain William Clark 37.
(10) Lewis and Clark, History of the Expedition Under the Command of Lewis and Clark (Coues) 818-819.
(11) Letter Donald Jackson to author. January 22, 1968.
(12) A color reproduction of this painting appears in Andrist, To The Pacific With Lewis and Clark 139.
(13) Jackson, Letters of the Lewis and Clark Expedition 424.
(14) Hicks 25-6.
(14a) The collection of Thomas E. Holt includes a specimen, 1805 dated lockplate, with serial number 1520.
(15) Sawyer 131.
(16) Hicks II 36.
(17) Ibid. 134.
(18) Gurney 12.
(19) Hicks 47.
(20) Ibid. 48.
(21) Greenleaf's Point, also known as Arsenal Point, is the present site of Fort McNair and the National War College. Green, Washington Village and Capitol 3 and 91.
(22) Patterson 24.
(23) Memorandum to author. May 1968.
(24) Metschl 119.
(25) American Rifleman, August 1962, p. 19.
(26) Sawyer 132.
(27) Kimball Catalogue 7, Item HF1.
(28) Sawyer 132.

Collection of Edwin and Robert Bitter.

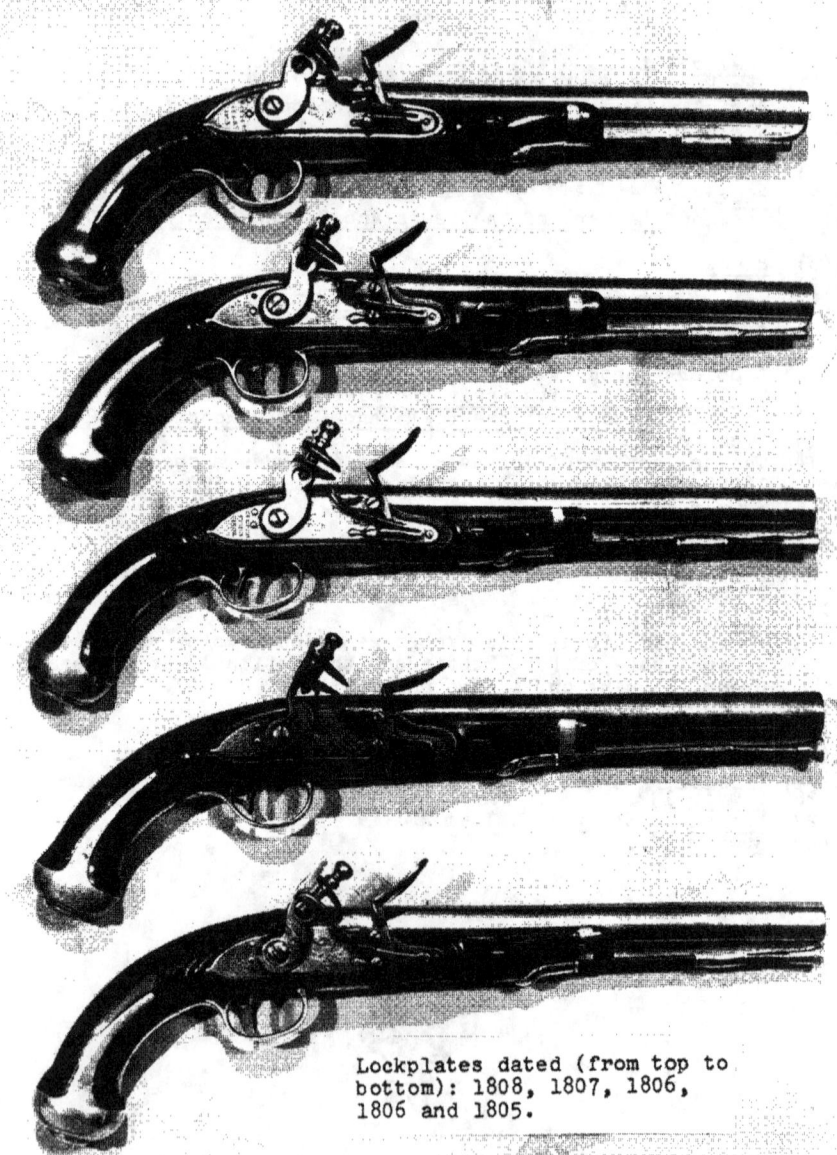

Lockplates dated (from top to bottom): 1808, 1807, 1806, 1806 and 1805.

See, also, page 156.

III. THE EARLY PISTOLS

Pistols Pre-Dating the Model 1806 (?)

James A. Smith and Elmer Swanson, in <u>The Antique Pistol Book</u>, describe and depict by a drawing (see below) a Harpers Ferry pistol with an 1804 dated lockplate.

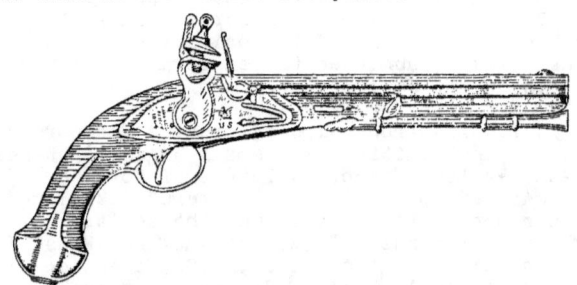

FIG. 178 - HARPERS FERRY, .54 cal., 10 inch octagon rifled steel barrel, with barrel rib, 3/4 length walnut stock with ball butt and tang plate, barrel bar fastened to stock, gooseneck double legged hammer, brass mountings. Marked "Eagle U.S. Harpers Ferry" and date on lock. This was the first rifled pistol barrel manufactured by the U.S. Government. Length overall 15-3/4 inches.

Swanson advises that the illustration and description were copied from a dealer's catalogue.

The writer of this study has never seen such a pistol, and does not know of anyone who has ever seen such a pistol.

Van Rensselear describes a Harpers Ferry "Army pistol calibre .36, 10 in. octagon barrel, brass mounted, half stock", and at least implies that it pre-dates the Model 1806. (1)

The writer of this study has never seen such a pistol, and does not know of anyone who has ever seen such a pistol.

Model 1806

"* * * the most graceful and handsome of all United States martial flintlock pistols * * *"

On November 13, 1805, Secretary of War Henry Dearborn instructed Superintendent Joseph Perkin of Harpers Ferry to "make arrangements for, and commencing making, horsemen's pistols", and to manufacture from 500 to 1000 pairs per year until 2000 pairs were completed.

Some time prior to February 26, 1806, Perkin made and dispatched to Dearborn two pairs of pistols, and Dearborn wrote to Perkin on that date, stating that he considered "those with half stock and ribs, as entitled to a decided preference", but directed that there be "the addition of a small brass sight near the muzzle". (2)

The collection of Edwin Bitter and Robert Bitter contains an 1805 dated specimen with serial number M 2. The specimen is probably either one of the pair of model half stock pistols that Perkin submitted to Dearborn or an armory duplicate that was retained at Harpers Ferry.

As regards front sights, despite Dearborn's direction that there be "the addition of a small brass sight near the muzzle", and despite Dearborn's letter of November 3, 1807, wherein he advised Coxe that the "pattern" pistol made at Harpers Ferry "requires no alteration except the addition of a small brass sight near the muzzle" (3), most of the Model 1806's do not have front sights. A specimen, 1806 dated lockplate, serial number 50, in the collection of Samuel E. Smith has a silver blade front sight and a German silver oval insert in the wrist of the stock. (4)

The Bomford production records show that only eight pistols were made at Harpers Ferry in 1806, and that these were patterns. But Lieutenant Colonel R. C. Kuhn advises that Harpers Ferry was then operating on a fiscal year basis, running from October 1st to September 30th, and that the first quarter of 1807 was October, November and December of 1806.

According to Lieutenant Colonel Kuhn, the pistol production in 1806, et seq. , was as follows:

```
1807 (1st Quarter) dated 1806 - eight
     pattern pistols    464 pistols
1807 (2nd Quarter)      900 pistols
1807 (3rd Quarter)      668 pistols
1807 (4th Quarter)      848 pistols
1808 (1st Quarter - October, November
     and December of 1807) (dated 1807)
     920 pistols
1808 (2nd Quarter)      288 pistols   (5)
```

Samuel E. Smith has, for the past thirty-six years, been compiling a list of serial numbers of Model 1806's, and he advises that the lowest and highest numbers shown on his list of 266 pistols are as follows:

On pistols with lockplates dated 1806, the lowest serial number is 4 (present location of pistol not known - - -

formerly in the collection of the late David L. Ingalls, a collection that was sold in 1940 by the Far West Hobby Shop), and the highest serial number is 212 (present location of pistol not known - - - formerly in the collection of the late Richard T. Brady).

A dealer's catalogue lists a specimen with an 1806 dated lockplate with serial number 358 (6), but this serial number appears to be out of order. Samuel E. Smith's list includes serial numbers 203 and 209 with 1806 dated lockplates, but the interval between 212 and 358 is rather large.

On pistols with lockplates dated 1807, the lowest serial number is 62 (collection of the late Chauncey Hawthorne). Samuel E. Smith's list includes eleven pistols with lockplates dated 1807 and with serial numbers greater than 62 but less than 212. The two serial numbers next above 62 are 102 and 107, and the indications are that serial number 62 is out of order. Samuel E. Smith's lists also includes a second pistol with serial number 212 (also formerly in the collection of the late Richart T. Brady) but with a lockplate dated 1807.

On pistols with lockplates dated 1807, the highest serial number is 1966 (collection of Dr. Thomas B. Snyder).

On pistols with lockplates dated 1808, the lowest serial number is 61, which appears to be out of order, as does serial number 758 on the pistol with an 1808 dated lockplate "that Harry Berry turned up in an attic in Baltimore". Samuel E. Smith expresses the opinion that the "real series" (for 1808) begins with serial number 1592. On pistols with lockplates dated 1808, the highest serial number is 2048 - - - and the production record total (4096) is exactly twice this number.

Samuel E. Smith's lists shows (and he concludes) that there is no "clean cutoff" in the lockplate dates and serial numbers. Apparently, the assemblers either did not exhaust the supply of lockplates dated in one year before beginning to use lockplates dated in the subsequent year or did not use barrels in the order of their serial numbers.

- - - - - - - - - - - - - - - - - -

The Model 1806 is Caliber .54, has an overall length of 16 in., weighs approximately 2 lbs. 9 oz., and has a barrel that is approximately 10 in. long.

The specimen, 1806 dated lockplate, shown on the rear of the jacket is in the collection of J. Garnand Hamilton.

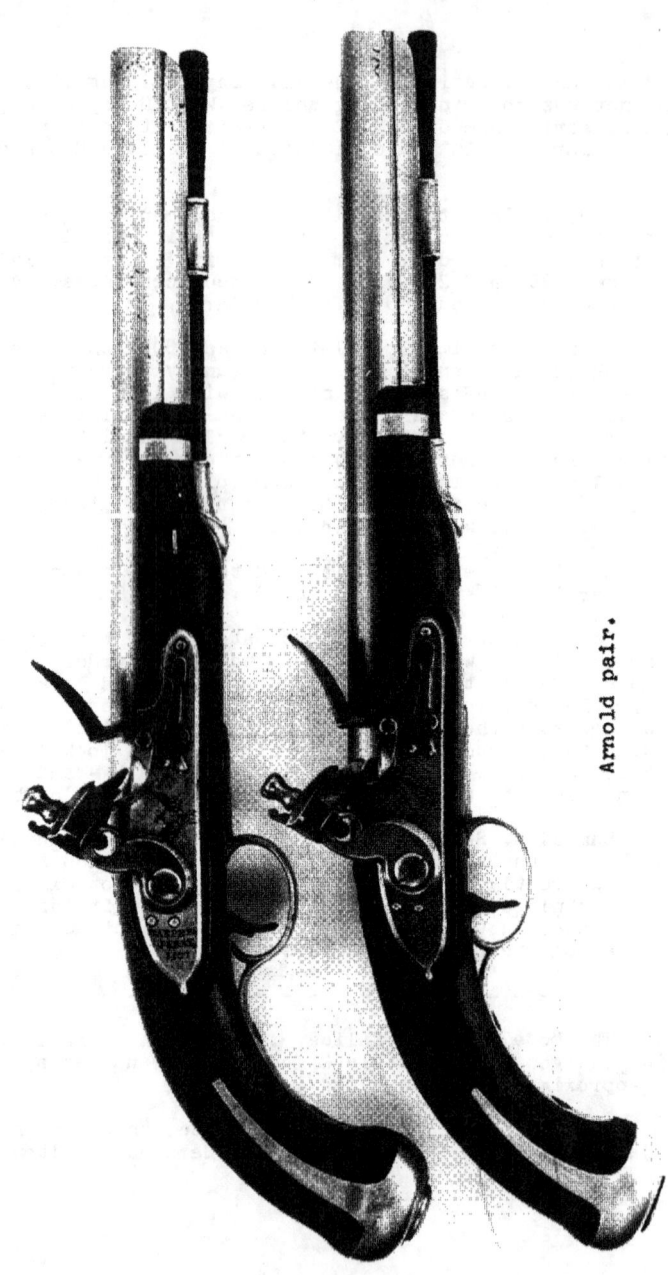

Arnold pair.

A specimen, 1806 dated lockplate, is described as having a "V" stamped on the inside of the lockplate, and an "I" stamped on the lower right side of the butt. (7)

Pairs

A pair, serial numbers 351, 1807 dated lockplates, are in the collection of Ralph E. Arnold. The photographs of this pair show clearly the handmade, non-interchangeable character of the early Harpers Ferry arms, and variations that are attributable to hand manufacture as well as to differences in material. The photographs show variations in the length of the butt cap extensions, in the width of the brass bands near the tail pipes, and in the distance from the bands to the tail pipes. The length and shape of the trigger guard straps differ slightly, and the locks are not interchangeable. "WV" is stamped on the inside of the lockplates (similar to the "V" on the specimen with the 1806 dated lockpalte noted in the preceding paragraph), and there are three parallel file marks on the side lock screws, wedges, and brass side plates; there are three similar marks cut into the stock under the side plates, and into the original wooden ramrods near the small ends; and there are three similar chisel marks on the undersides of the barrels (near the breech), and on the tangs.

The "V" over "CW" stamped on the stock are the inspector's marks of Charles Williams. A "4" over the letter "R" is stamped on the right side of the butt of each arm, and similar markings but with different numbers and letters have been reported in the same position on other specimens. See page 157.

Another pair reported by Samuel E. Smith, in addition to the serial number 212 Brady pair mentioned above, is presently owned by Dr. James Lucie (serial number 2038). And Samuel E. Smith advises that there is still another pair, making a total of four pairs presently known to him.

- - - - - - - - - - - - - - - -

The lockplates on Model 1806's vary at least from 4 3/4 in. to 4.87 in. in length, and from 7/8 in. to 1 in. in width, and even greater variations may exist.

The iron pans on all of the Model 1806's are forged integrally with the lockplates.

The Bitter specimen, 1808 dated lockplate, has a rifled barrel similar to that of the Model 1804 Rifle, but the writer of this study does not know of any other Model 1806 Pistols that have rifled barrels.

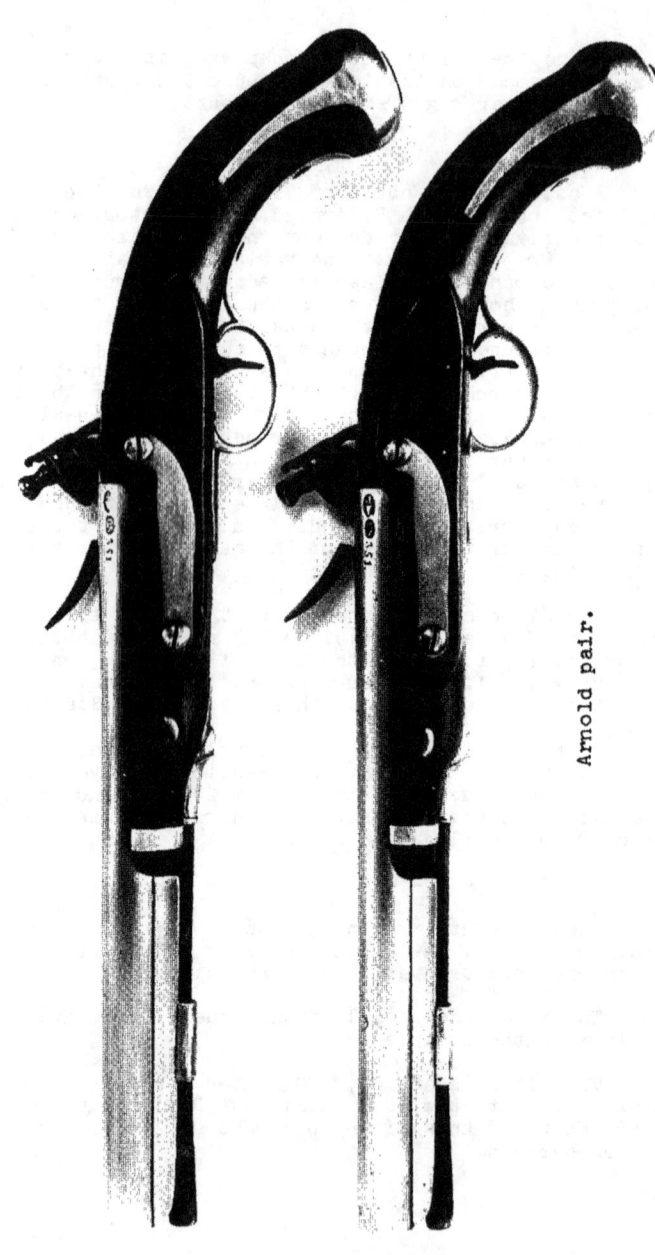

Arnold pair.

A few of the Model 1806's have rear sights, but apparently, these sights were added at a date later than that of the pistol's manufacture.

Steel ramrods (swell tipped) are found on some specimens, but the probabilities are that all of the original ramrods were hickory with a brass tip for loading, and with an iron tip at the other end, the iron tip being slotted to hold a cleaning rag. The brass tips vary in design.

The ramrod pipe is iron, and the tail pipe is brass.

All of the mountings are brass, and the rear end of the trigger guard strap is round.

A pair of Model 1806's is reported with dove tail rear sights set into the barrels, but with no proof or inspector's marks whatsoever. One of the pair has a lockplate dated 1807, and serial number 675, and the other has a lockplate dated 180<u>3</u>, and serial number 1680 (which indicates that it was probably made ca. 1808). (8)

On January 1, 1810, there were on hand at Harpers Ferry, "fit for service", 4022 "Pistols (Horseman's) marked Harpers Ferry". (9)

A rather poor quality Belgian reproduction of a specimen with an 1807 dated lockplate is presently being retailed for $69.50. Some persons have "antiqued" their purchases.

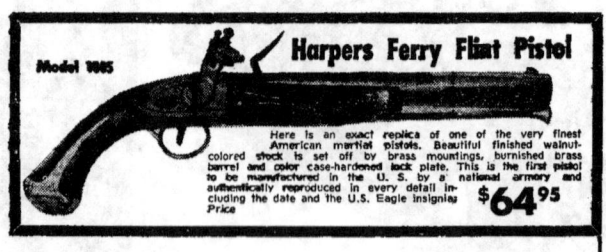

51

On April 17, 1922, a pair of crossed Model 1806's was approved as the official insignia of the United States Military Police, the thought being that if Model 1806's rather than current pistols were chosen, they would not become outmoded. (10)

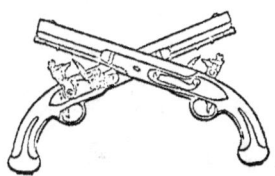

Patterns for North Model 1811 (?)

By letter dated December 4, 1810, Secretary of War William Eustis wrote to Tench Coxe, Purveyor of Supplies, in part, as follows:

> "A number of Harpers Ferry pistols have been ordered to Phila. by Mr. Irvine who will deliver you three or four for patterns.
>
> "The handle or grip of these pistols appear to be too small and a little too short as Mr. North will describe to you." (11)

Patterns for North Model 1813

On December 8, 1812, Eustis wrote to Stubblefield directing that Harpers Ferry make six pattern pistols "conformably to the enclosed drawing & the directions of Mr. Wickham" (12), and the Bomford production records show that four pattern pistols were produced in fiscal 1812.

Patterns for North Model 1816 (?)

James A. Smith and Elmer Swanson, in The Antique Pistol Book, describe and depict by a drawing (see below) a Harpers Ferry pistol with an 1814 dated lockplate.

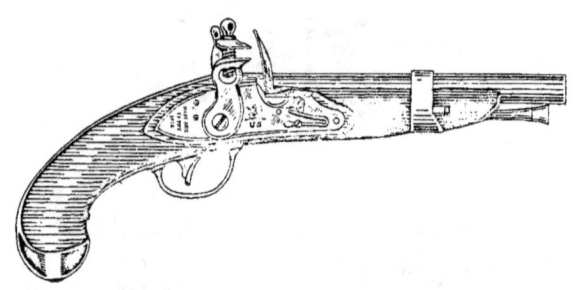

FIG. 180 - HARPERS FERRY, .54 cal., 10-1/2 inch round steel barrel, smooth bore, walnut stock, steel mountings, barrel bar fastened with fore-end band, round ball butt with back strap and trigger guard strap. Marked "Eagle U.S., Harpers Ferry" with date. Heavy military double legged flat hammer. Length overall 15-1/2 inches.

Swanson advises that the illustration and description were copied from a dealer's catalogue.

Van Rensselear describes a Harpers Ferry pistol with an 1814 dated lockplate "calibre .54, 9 1/8 - inch round barrel, length 15 1/2 inches * * * quite similar to the Model 1816 North * * * only three are known". (13)

The writer of this study has never seen a Harpers Ferry pistol with an 1814 dated lockplate.

But by letter dated June 10, 1815, Wadsworth expressed the opinion that United States pistols should be of rifle caliber (.54) "for greater simplicity", and that it was "essentially wrong * * * to give a pistol the same caliber as a musket". (14) The North Model 1813 as well as the North Model 1811 were Caliber .69. And Wadsworth's statement in the same letter that "the pattern of the pistols made at Harpers Ferry I approve" could well be an indication that pattern pistols were made by Harpers Ferry in 1814.

Samuel E. Smith advises that, in Philadelphia, in about 1912, a pistol was made using a Harpers Ferry rifle lock, including an 1814 dated lockplate, and using a North 1816 Pistol with a cut down stock, a new barrel band, and several other "refinements". (15)

Model 1819 (patterns)

By letter dated March 2, 1819, Wadsworth wrote to Stubblefield:

"I received the Pistols by Mr. McGuire, the pair with brown barrels I like best. The middle band I think unnecessary and wish you to make another Pair Similar to them, omitting the middle band, and making such other alterations as I am now to suggest. The upper band to be polished as well as the side plate, which makes a better finish than blueing. The ramrod & swivel to be polished, the Guard and Breech tang to be browned, the heads of the side pins to be flat and polished as likewise the head of the Tang screw.

"The Caliber of the Pistol ought to be such as to receive a Rifle Ball weighing half an ounce when made into a Paper cartridge. Therefore it should be a trifle larger in the bore than the Rifle, but the Cartridge ought to fit very snugly else when the Pistol is loaded and placed in the Holster muzzle downwards the Bullet will shift its place. You can adjust the caliber to a proper size by making up some cartridges with Rifle balls. I intend this Pattern as a Model to be worked after in some Contracts we expect to make. Therefor wish half a dozen pair made and Sent to me, as early as convenient. The handle or Grasp of the Stock is a little longer than necessary." (16)

Then, on June 12, 1819, contractor Simeon North acknowledged receipt of "a pair of Pattern Pistols". (17)

The specimen in the Locke collection (page 54) is apparently one of the pistols with the "middle band" that Wadsworth referred to (and rejected) in his letter to Stubblefield of March 2, 1819. It has "U.S." stamped on the butt cap below the union with the back strap.

A later specimen - - - it has no "middle band" - - - is described as being an "exact pattern" of the North Model 1819. (18) It has an overall length of 15 1/2 in., and a barrel

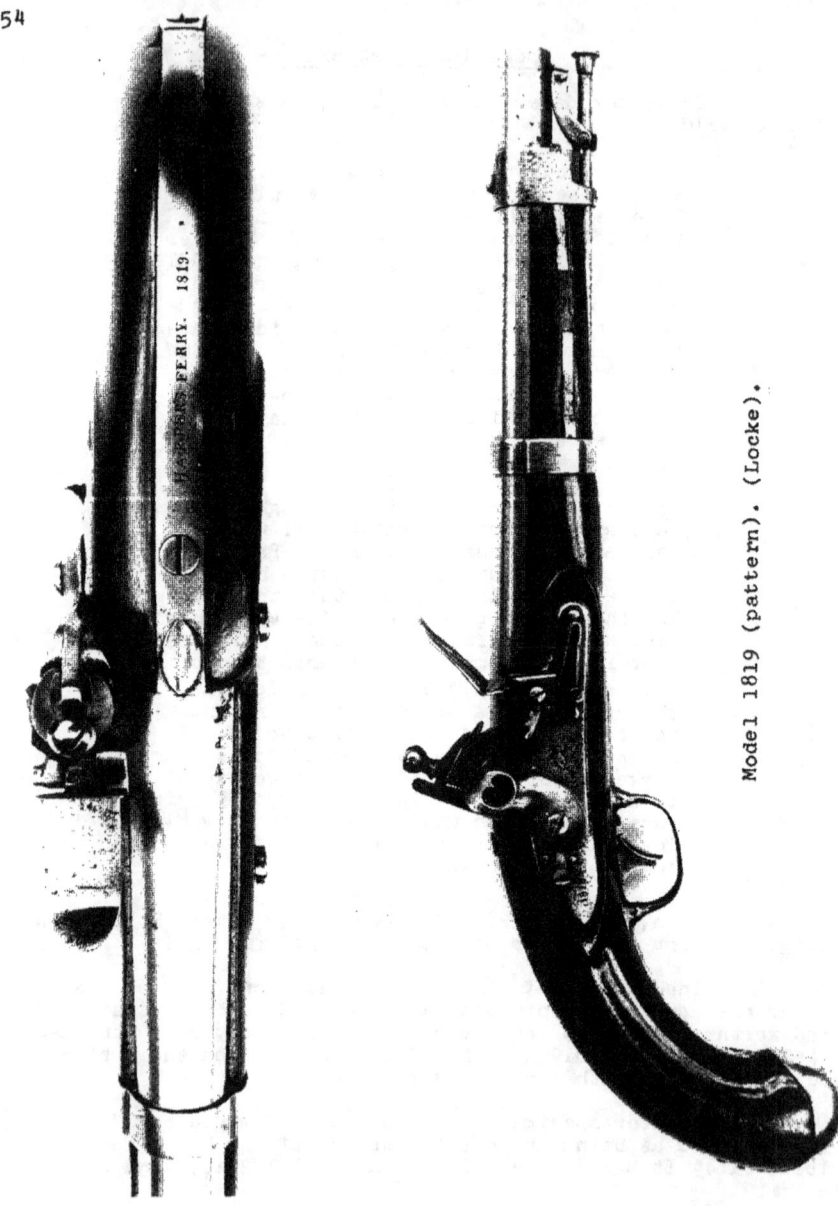

Model 1819 (pattern). (Locke).

that is 10 in. long, and has flat breech sides. The pistol has a sliding safety bolt (as does the Locke specimen), and the lockplate and the barrel markings are the same as those on the Locke specimen, except that all parts of the later pistol are marked "2". Photographs of the later pistol (converted to percussion) appear on pages 28 and 29 of Gun Report for October of 1965 (Vol. XI, No. 5). Nomenclature of parts of the pistol (as given by Benjamin Moore of Harpers Ferry on August 29, 1839) is set out in the same issue of Gun Report on pages 30 and 31. Moore, on the same date, wrote that two pistols had been made at Harpers Ferry in 1819.

Thus, it seems that of the six (or three pair) of pattern pistols made at Harpers Ferry in 1819, one pair had brown barrels and "middle" bands, one pair had "middle" bands but did not have brown barrels, and one pair (the approved patterns) did not have "middle" bands.

Model 1836 (patterns) (?)

A dealer's catalogue gives the following listing: "Model pistol for contractors of 1836. Exactly resembles these made by Johnson & Waters, but lock is stamped only with Springfield or Harpers Ferry eagle, so it was doubtless made as a pattern for contractors to follow". (19)

Notes

(1) Van Rensselear 111.
(2) Hicks 26.
(3) Hicks II 17.
(4) Letter Samuel E. Smith to author. April 30, 1968.
(5) Letter Lt. Col. R. C. Kuhn to author. March 31, 1968.
(6) Jackson Catalogue 20.
(7) Gun Report Vol. III, No. 12 (May 1958) p. 65.
(8) Texas Gun Collector No. 51. (October 1954) p. 18.
(9) Hicks II 134.
(10) Letter Colonel Ed V. Hendren, Jr., The Institute of Heraldry, United States Army, to author. February 1, 1968.
(11) Hicks. 37.
(12) Ibid. 39.
(13) Van Rensselear 111.
(14) Gluckman 406.
(15) Letters to author. April 30, 1968, and May 28, 1968. Smith cites correspondence dated from 1912 to 1924 between George C. Maynard, Curator, Division of Mechanical Technology, Smithsonian, and Jerome Clark, and David L. Ingalls.
(16) Gun Report Vol. XI, No. 5 (October 1965) p. 26.
(17) Hicks 60.
(18) Patterson, "The Harpers Ferry 1819".
(19) Kimball Catalogue 6, Item 208.

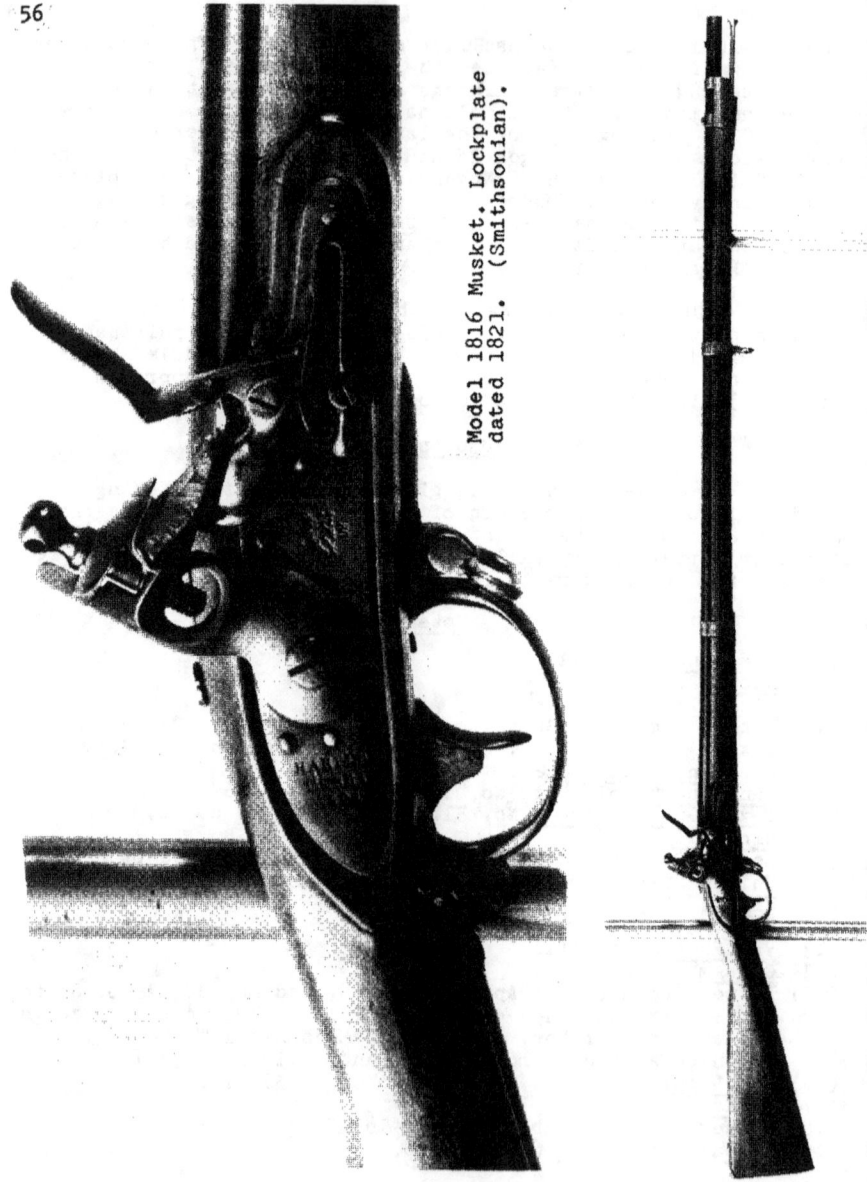

Model 1816 Musket. Lockplate dated 1821. (Smithsonian).

IV. THE 1816-1822 SERIES

Model 1816 Musket

Following the hectic days of the War of 1812 (that ended in January of 1815 with the Battle of New Orleans), a serious effort was made to standarize United States arms. Sometime prior to June 10, 1815, Decius Wadsworth, Colonel of Ordnance, "discoursed" with Lieutenant Colonel Roswell Lee, the Springfield Superintendent; with Benjamin Prescott, Lee's predecessor; with James Stubblefield, the Harpers Ferry Superintendent; and with Eli Whitney (1765-1825) the inventor of the cotton gin, and a pioneer in United States efforts to produce firearms with interchangeable parts. (1)

In 1815, American firearms were, for the most part, hand made, one at a time. Production was slow (only skilled artisans could be used), armory repairs were costly, and repairs in the field were often impossible.

France, "that warlike nation", had progressed towards achieving the goal of parts interchangeability - - - in a letter written from Paris in August 30, 1785, Thomas Jefferson, Minister to France, reported to John Jay, Secretary of Foreign Affairs:

"An improvement is made here in the construction of the musket which it may be interesting to Congress to know, should they at any time propose to procure any. It consists in the making every part of them so exactly alike that what belongs to any one, may be used for every other musket in the magazine. The government here has examined and approved the method, and is establishing a large manufactory for the purpose. As yet the inventor has only completed the lock of the musket on this plan. He will proceed immediately to have the barrel, stock, and their parts executed in the same way. Supposing it might be useful to the U.S., I went to the workman, he presented me the parts of 50 locks, taken to pieces, and arranged in compartments. I put several together myself taking pieces at hazard as they came to hand, and they fitted in the most perfect manner. The advantages of this, when arms need repair, are evident. He effects it by tools of his own contrivance which at the same time abridge the work so that he thinks he shall be able to furnish the musket two livres cheaper than the common price. But it will be two or three years before he will be able to furnish any quantity. I mention it now, as it may have influence on the plan for furnishing our magazines with this arm". (2)

Le Blanc's improvement "took very limited hold in France * * * while in England it was solely applied to lowering the costs of the pulleys made for the navy. In America, however, it was applied to the mass production of more and more objects - - - clocks and watches, hardware and sewing machines - - - because it solved the shortage of workers". (3)

Jefferson encouraged Whitney to strive towards parts interchangeability - - - from France, he sent Whitney a French Model 1777 Musket - - - and perhaps as early as 1801, with the approval of the Ordnance Board, Whitney incorporated into the United States muskets made at his Connecticutt plant several French improvements including a separable brass pan that did not have a fence (and tilted upward in the rear), a rounded cock, and a frizzen with a flared head, and a cut off toe. (4)

Wadsworth's "discourse" with Whitney, et al., disclosed no "material discordance of opinion * * * relative to the essential properties and dimensions of firearms", and as one result of the discourse, Wadsworth directed that both Harpers Ferry and Springfield produce one or more models for a new type of musket. By letter dated November 23, 1816, Wadsworth advised Lee that the model produced by Springfield had been adopted, and that this Springfield model was then at Harpers Ferry "where a number will be made as exactly conformable to it as practicable". And in the same letter, Wadsworth stated that he would direct an annual exchange between Harpers Ferry and Springfield of a case of arms so "that by comparing them together it might be seen wherein the work of the two Armories disagree, in order that proper measures might be taken to render the work quite uniform". (5)

At long last, the day was dawning when there would be reasonable similarity between the products of Harpers Ferry and those of Springfield, and by December 15, 1821, Lee (in a letter addressed to Stubblefield) was speaking of a "quarterly interchange of muskets". (6)

In the Model 1816, the old musket caliber (.69) is retained, the stock is larger and longer, the barrel is shortened to 42 in., and there are a number of changes to conform the lock more closely to that of the French Model 1777, the main lock change being in the use of a separable brass pan that does not have a fence, and that tilts upward in the rear.

The Smithsonian specimen, 1821 dated lockplate, measures 57 11/16 in. overall, has a 54 in. stock, and weighs 9 lbs. 6 oz., and these dimensions and this weight seem to be representative.

The interior parts of the lock of the Model 1816 are of a much better construction and finish than are those of the earlier muskets (a result of better machinery). The lockplate is case hardened, and is flat and has a bevel edge in the front (projecting slightly from the stock), but the rear is round, and curves to a point. The lockplate measures 6 5/8 in. by 1 5/16 in. (However, the old, flat face lockplate and the flat face cock were used until sometime in 1819 when Harpers Ferry first began to produce muskets with the inclined, detachable brass pan, and the rounded cock.) (7)

The cock has a round surface, and the top of the frizzen is bent forward to facilitate the fall of the flint. The top end of the frizzen spring curls down slightly.

The 54 in. stock has no comb.

The stock of the Smithsonian specimen is stamped on the left side opposite the lock "AB" in script in an oval (for Armistead Beckham), and "V" over "PH" in Roman letters (for viewed-Phillip Hoffman). And "JS" (for James Stubblefield) is stamped in Roman letters on the stock just behind the rear end of the trigger guard plate.

The barrel markings vary widely. Although the "V", "P" and an eagle head (reading in that order, from front to rear) seem to be the most usual, the Smithsonian specimen has a "P" in an oval, an eagle head, and a "V", reading in that order, from front to rear.

The 2 1/8 in. barrel tang is dated, and on at least several specimens, the barrel tang date differs from that on the lockplate.

The breech plug is shortened to permit the passage (outside) of the rear lock bolt. There is a bayonet stud on the top of the barrel 1 1/4 in. from the muzzle.

There is a blade sight on the rear strap of the front band, but there is no rear sight.

The bayonet is marked "US", it weighs 11 3/4 oz., and is triangular with a 16 in. blade, 1 in. wide at the bottom of its widest face. The blade is hollow ground from the point rearward for 9 in., and the 3 in. socket has no locking band.

The ramrod is steel.

The furniture is iron. The rear band and the middle band are retained by band springs forward of the bands. The front band is 2 3/8 in. long, with two straps, each being 1/2 in. wide. The middle band is 11/16 in. wide, and carries the riveted front sling swivel. The rear band is 5/8 in. wide at the top, and 1 1/4 in. wide at the bottom.

The butt plate, marked "US" on the heel, is 4 3/8 in. by 2 in. The trigger guard bow is riveted to the 9 3/4 in. trigger guard plate.

Wadsworth, following his "discourse" with the experts, recommended that barrels be browned (8), and sometime prior to April 5, 1820, the Ordnance Department came "to a determination to brown the muskets". (9) By that date, Springfield had "commenced the process", and the probabilities are that Harpers Ferry was doing likewise. Also, the probabilities are that only the barrel was being browned, but on or about April 27, 1821, the Ordnance Department determined to brown the following: barrel, bands, swivels, sideplate, tang of the breech pin, bayonet, band springs, guard, trigger plate, and heel plate. The screws, guard screws, side pins, tang pin and trigger were "to be polished and case hardened, and left in that state". The ramrod was "to remain bright as heretofore", and the lock was to "remain as at present prescribed" (probably case hardened). (10)

The post-1821 arms thus browned are sometimes known as "national armory brown", and those made after 1831 (when browning was discontinued) are sometimes known as "national armory bright". (11)

Model 1822

In 1821, both of the national armories were directed to produce thirty models, and despite Bomford's statement that "no alteration * * * is intended by this arrangement", (12), the designation "Model 1822" soon became official - - - the designation "Model 1816" was apparently coined by collectors.

The models made by Harpers Ferry were selected as the types that were to be manufactured in the future by both public and private armories (13), and the only change in them (from the Model 1816's) is that the rear sling swivel is riveted to a slight protuberance at the front of the trigger guard bow rather than to a separate stud projecting from the trigger guard plate directly in front of the bow. In some later specimens, the rivet of the rear sling swivel passes through the center of the front of the trigger guard bow. See page

Sawyer reports conversions done in 1842 when the barrels were grooved, and rear sights were added, with the date of the conversion being stamped on the breech. He also reports 1854 conversions that "consisted in reducing the calibre to the prevailing one of .58 by brazing a lining tube in the barrel". (14) Other conversions involved the installation of new breeches with integrally cast cone bolsters. (14a)

The Nunnemacher Collection includes an 1837 dated specimen with the Butterfield conversion. The words "Butterfield's Patent Dec. 11, 1855. Philada." are stamped in front of the hammer, and most parts of the gun are marked "98", with some parts being marked "2". (14b)

Harpers Ferry continued to make the Model 1822 musket until at least 1843, and perhaps as late as 1844. (15)

Model 1822's were the standard shoulder arms of Lieutenant Charles Wilkes' South Sea Exploring Expedition (1838-48), and on some occasions, they were used for gifts and as barter. (16)

Model 1816 Musket (Artillery)

In 1817, Captain Partridge, in charge of the cadets at West Point, wrote to Wadsworth, stating that the "standard muskets are too heavy in general" for the cadets, and asking for shorter arms. Wadsworth, for "sometimes past", had contemplated a "consignment of that nature, in order to save much of the barrels as may burst or prove defective near the muzzle", and on January 29, 1817, he ordered Springfield to make up some 36 in. barrel muskets, but not more than ten in a hundred, "nor more than may take up the barrels which prove too short for standard muskets". (17)

"For distinction's sake", these short arms were to be called "Artillery Muskets".

Partridge also requested that the cadet arms be "considerably lighter", but Wadsworth ruled that the Artillery Muskets

Model 1822 Musket. Conversion. New breech with integrally cast cone bolster. (Brown).

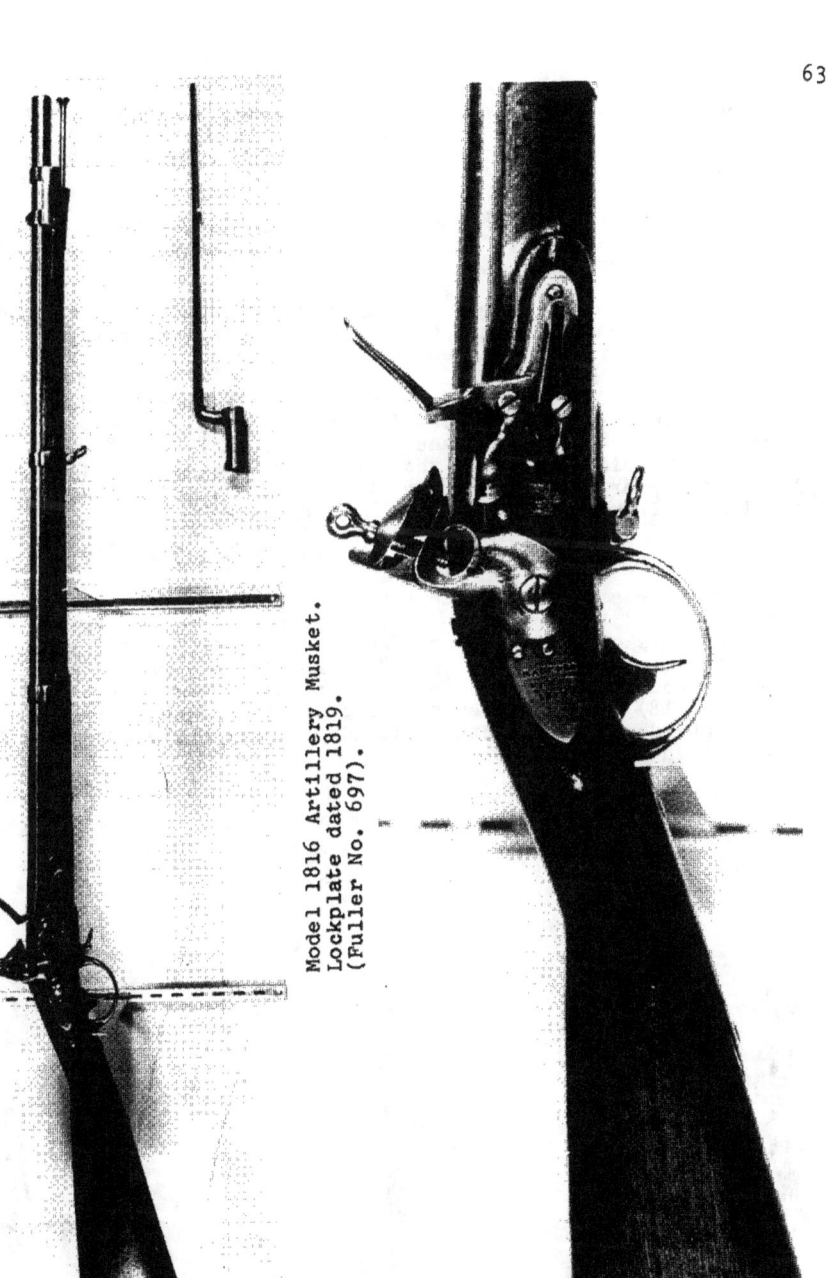

Model 1816 Artillery Musket.
Lockplate dated 1819.
(Fuller No. 697).

be standard (except, of course, for the shorter length), and acceded only to the extent of stating that "it may not be amiss to choose (from standard parts) the locks with lighter springs and the lighted bayonets".

       The Artillery Muskets, according to Lieutenant Colonel Lee of Springfield were "well calculated" for the Marines as well as the Artillery.

       Was Harpers Ferry also authorized to use up its "barrels which prove too short", and to make as many as ten Artillery Muskets for every one hundred standard muskets manufactured?

       There is a Harpers Ferry specimen with an 1819 dated lockplate in the Fuller Collection (see page 63). The top of the barrel is marked "V", "P", and an eagle head, "I", "48", and "1819". The distances from the breech to the bands are: 10 3/8 in. to the rear band, 20 3/8 in. to the middle band, and 30 5/8 in. to the front band. The arm has a brass pan.

- - - - - - - - - - - - - - - - - - -

       By letter dated September 3, 1821, Bomford wrote to Lee, recalling that the purpose of authorizing the 36 in. barrel Artillery Musket was to arm the West Point cadets, and revoking the authorization, stating that "the number of short muskets, already made, is greater than will ever be required by the cadets". (18) And the probabilities are that if Harpers Ferry was authorized to manufacture Artillery Muskets, its authorization was revoked at the same time.

Model 1819 Rifle

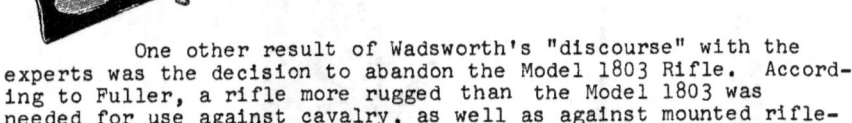

One other result of Wadsworth's "discourse" with the experts was the decision to abandon the Model 1803 Rifle. According to Fuller, a rifle more rugged than the Model 1803 was needed for use against cavalry, as well as against mounted riflemen. (19)

By 1817, Marine T. Wickham, Chief Armorer at Harpers Ferry, produced a model for this new full stock "Standard Rifle". Nine patterns were produced at Harpers Ferry in 1818, and two more patterns were produced there in 1819. (20) Apparently, the model and the patterns all had lockplates dated 1817 - - - Lewis advises that he has not seen any Harpers Ferry Model 1819 Rifles that did not have 1817 dated lockplates, and that were not marked "Model" or "M". (21) He further expresses a doubt that Harpers Ferry ever made any general issue Model 1819 Rifles (and in this expression, the writer of this study concurs).

The Model 1819 is often referred to as "the Common Rifle", but although the Model 1819 is a "Common Rifle", the Model 1819 is not the, i.e., the only "Common Rifle". After the advent of the definitely uncommon Hall rifle in 1819, every other United States rifle was a "common rifle", and was classified as either "half or whole stock". The Model 1803 was a "common rifle", and even the Model 1841 was officially called a "common rifle". (22)

Sawyer concludes that the workmanship on the exterior and on the lock "rivals that of a fine sporting rifle" although the interior of the barrel is but little, if any, better than that of the preceding model; but there is a formed chamber which possibly is a slight improvement". (23)

The arm's overall length is 51 1/2 in., and including the bayonet, it weighs 10 1/4 lbs.

The old rifle caliber (.54), and the old barrel length (36 in.) are retained. The lockplate, similar to, but smaller than that of the Model 1816 Musket, measures 5 1/2 in. by 1 3/16 in.

The stock is 48 in. long.

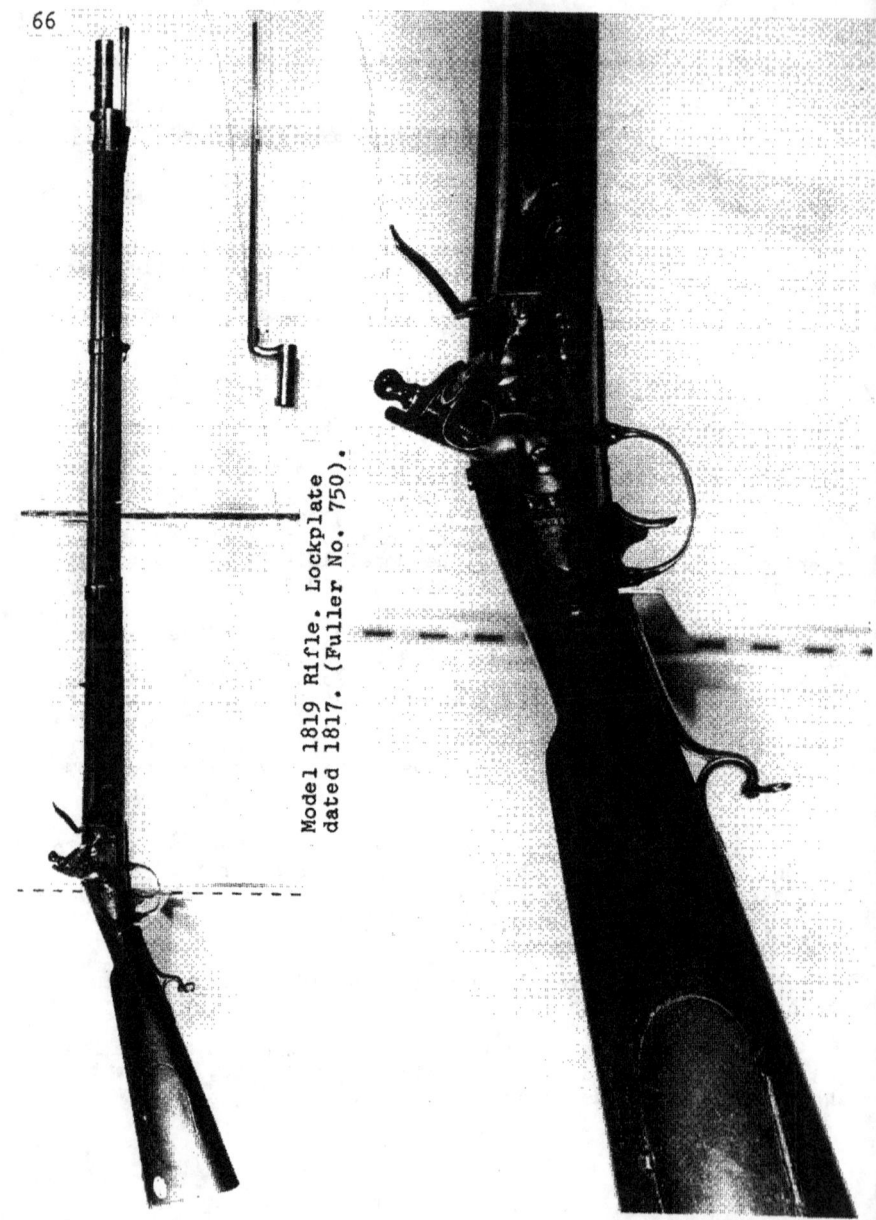

Model 1819 Rifle. Lockplate dated 1817. (Fuller No. 750).

The barrel is round, and the bore is heptagonal, with seven narrow grooves at the apices. The grooves are .01 in. deep, and make ont turn in 50 in.

The sights are similar to those of the Model 1803 Rifle.

Apparently, the early Model 1819's were not originally equipped with bayonets, (24), but the Fuller specimen (page 66) has a bayonet lug, and a blade front sight on the front strap of the front band.

The furniture is iron.

The brass-tipped, steel ramrod has a cup end, and the opposite end is threaded.

The wood is not filled, but is treated with severl coats of linseed oil. The brass pan is polished, the ramrod is finished bright, and all other metal (iron or steel) parts are heat blued, except for the barrel (which is browned), and the frizzen (which is case hardened, gray).

The patch box was furnished with a paper wrapped parcel containing a wormer to screw on the ramrod, a combination screw driver with a lever for turning the jaw screw, and a piece of machine-stamped sheet lead called a "flint cap". (25)

Notes

(1) Gluckman 404.
(2) Jefferson, Papers of Thomas Jefferson. Vol. 8, p. 455.
(3) Mirsky and Nevins, World of Eli Whitney 221.
(4) Russell 151; and Fuller, Whitney Firearms 175.
(5) Hicks 51.
(6) Ibid. 54.
(7) Patterson 27.
(8) Gluckman 404.
(9) Hicks 53.
(10) Ibid.
(11) Regulations for the Government of the Ordnance Department (1834) 64.
(12) Hicks 53. In 1843, "good and servicable arms made from 1821 to 1831 inclusive" were classified as "suitable for alteration to percussion" - - - those made "from 1821 to 1831 inclusive" were not "considered suitable for ordinary issue, nor for alteration to percussion". Gluckman 402. A similar cut-off was made in the Regulations for the Government of the Ordnance Department (1834), page 57, where it is provided that "no muskets, rifles, or pistols, which have been manufactured at the Springfield or Harpers Ferry

Armories since the 1st of January, 1820 * * * will be issued from the national armories or ordnance stations in time of peace, either to the troops of the United States, or to the militia, without special instructions from the Secretary of War".

(13) Hicks 56.
(14) Sawyer 147-48.
(14a) The collection of Stuart E. Brown, III, contains a specimen, 1823 dated lockplate, with the barrel marked only with "421" (just forward of the replaced breech), and with the same number stamped inside the lock and on the stock (below the front end of the lock).
(14b) Charles W. Moore Catalogue 39, Item 39 is a Butterfield conversion with an 1836 dated lockplate.
(15) Patterson 29.
(16) Patterson, "Firearms on the Wilkes Expedition".
(17) Hicks 57.
(18) Ibid. 58.
(19) Fuller, Whitney Firearms 127.
(20) Russell 182; and Sawyer 134.
(21) Letter to author. May 21, 1968.
(22) Lewis, "Older Service Weapons Given Wrong Designation"; and Lewis 56.
(23) Sawyer 133-134.
(24) Ibid. 134.
(25) Ibid. 134. See Lewis Plate 20.

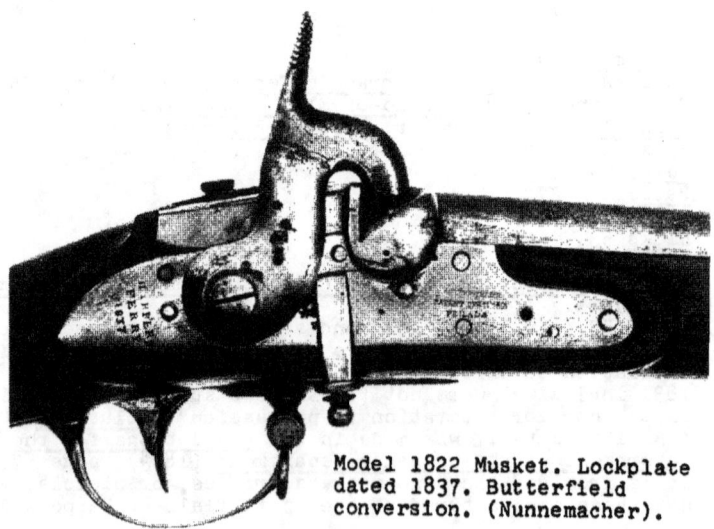

Model 1822 Musket. Lockplate dated 1837. Butterfield conversion. (Nunnemacher).

V. THE HALL ARMS

John Harris Hall, born in Portland, Maine, on January 21, 1778, was apprenticed at an early age to a boat builder in nearby Yarmouth. Later, Hall designed and built the "Yankee", an unconventional sloop with a flat bottom and a very deep keel that foundered on her maiden voyage, probably because of the keel. (1)

Hall also designed and made breech-laoding flintlock rifles - - - he wrote "I invented the improvement in 1811, being at that time but little acquainted with rifles, and being perfectly ignorant of any method whatsoever of loading guns at the breech". (2)

On May 21, 1811, a patent was issued to Hall and to William Thornton (3), a Washington architect, whom President Madison had appointed to be the first salaried chief of the Patent Office, and who frequently feathered his own nest by issuing patents to himself - - - his sharing in the Hall rifle patent may well have been in part in exchange for services rendered in procuring the patent - - - but Thornton proved his worth to the public in 1814 when he persuaded the British who had captured Washington to spare the Patent Office from their torches.

Hall's earliest rifles were probably made at his shop on Richardson's Wharf in Portland (4) and in the summer of 1812, Hall demonstrated his rifle's accuracy by standing at the foot of Temple Street in Portland, and firing a ball through the weathervane of the old First Parish Church. (5)

During the War of 1812, Hall served as a lieutenant in the Portland militia (light infantry), possibly then acquiring his title of "Captain", and following the War, Hall resumed his efforts to sell to the United States Government his rifle as well as his ideas for making rifles on an assembly line basis with completely interchangeable parts. In 1816, Hall produced 100 rifles (6) which he sold to the Government in 1817, and which were then tested at Greenleaf's Point (near Washington).(7) And by contract dated March 18, 1819, the United States employed Hall to design and construct at Harpers Ferry the tools and machinery necessary for manufacturing Hall arms in quantity, and to supervise their manufacture.

Hall's breech loading rifle was revolutionary, but more important was his goal "to make every similar part of every gun so much alike that it will suit every gun, so that if a thousand guns were taken apart and their limbs thrown promiscuously together in one heap, they may be taken promiscuously from the heap and will all come right".

Hall recognized that "in the first instance", the production of arms with interchangeable parts would "probably prove expensive, yet ultimately it will prove most economical, and be attended with great advantages". (8)

At Harpers Ferry, Hall was assigned manufacturing space and a few rather run-down buildings located on several of the ten or so small Shenandoah River islands that bear the collective name "Island of Virginius" or, simply, "The Island".

And without doubt, Hall encountered many difficulties in making the necessary tools and machinery that would use machine methods and die forging rather than the formerly used methods of hand forging and hand filing - - - it was not until 1823, that Hall's rifles went into production at the "Rifle Works", a name that came to be used to distinguish Hall's buildings from those of the "Musket Factory" that were located on the Potomac River side of the Harpers Ferry peninsula.

In 1825, two companies of U. S. troops stationed at Fortress Monroe (where there was an arsenal) were armed with Hall rifles, and these soldiers were using the Hall rifles as late as 1827. (9)

In 1826, a Commission composed of James Carrington, Luther Sage, and James Bell inspected the Rifle Works, and tested its products for interchangeability. In a communication dated January 6, 1827, the Commissioners reported to George Bomford, Colonel of Ordnance, that they had requested Springfield to send to Harpers Ferry 100 rifles made by Hall at Harpers Ferry in 1824, and which, ever since, had been in storage at Springfield. At Harpers Ferry, at a testing point, these rifles were stripped, the receivers were disassembled, and the parts were scattered "promiscuously over a large joiner's work bench". Then, 100 stocks which had just been finished at the Rifle Works were brought to the testing point, and parts from the 100 rifles were put onto the new stocks, "the work having been repeatedly mixed and changed" by the Commissioners as well as by the Harpers Ferry workmen. As fast as the rifles were put together, they were handed to the Commissioners, who "minutely examined" them, and who "were unable to discover any inaccuracy in any of their parts fitting each other". The parts, the Commissioners continued, fitted "with as much accuracy and correctness as they did when on the stocks to which they originally belonged". And, the Commissioners expressed a "doubt whether the best workman that may be selected from any armory, with the aid of the best machines in the elsewhere, could, in a whole life, make a hundred rifles or muskets that would, after being promiscuously mixed together, fit each other with the exact nicety that is to be found in those manufactured by Hall". (10)

This drawing (1857) shows the Island of Virginius' pre-Civil War Industrial complex. The covered bridge spanning the Shenandoah River (center, far left) is long gone. The buildings (center right) facing the canal, and located to the right of the rear of the railroad train, and to the left of the canal's arched bridge are the "Rifle Works" from whence came the Hall arms, and the later rifles and rifle muskets. The Civil War and a succession of subsequent floods levelled all of the buildings shown on the drawing.

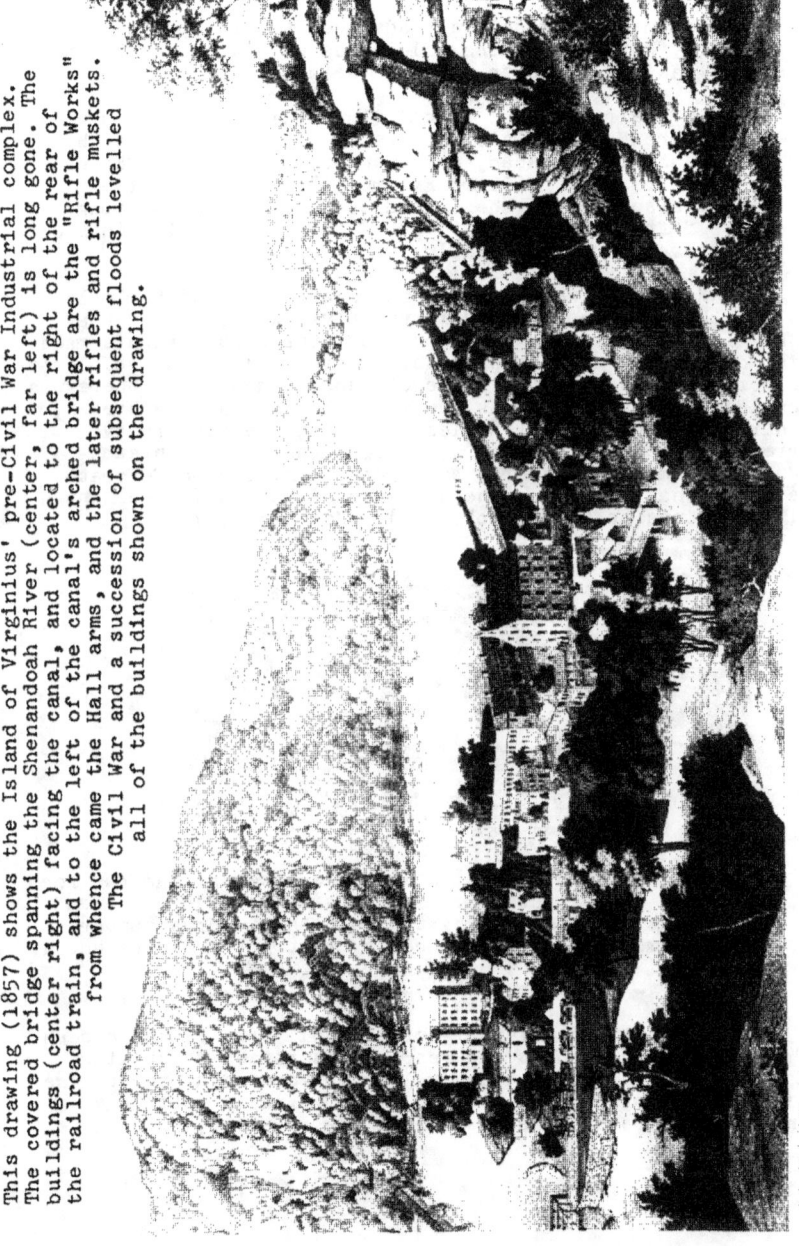

VIEW OF THE ISLAND VIRGINIUS, IN THE SHENANDOAH, AT HARPERS FERRY.

Whitney had made great advances towards parts interchangeability but Hall, whose tolerances were much smaller than Whitney's, was the first to achieve the goal.

In their day, the fast firing Hall arms were marvels - - - Commodore Matthew Calbraith Perry ("Old Bruin"), on his 1852-54 Expedition to Japan, presented to the Japanese Emperor on behalf of President Millard Fillmore "specimens of the articles manufactured in the United States", included among which were fifteen "Hall's Rifles", five of them being intended for the Emperor's own use. (11)

Hall arms were used in the Black Hawk and Seminole Wars, in the Mexican War, and in the Civil War. (12) But as far as field performance was concerned, the offset sights made aiming difficult, and the protruding lever galled the soldier's shoulder, and tangled with his equipment. Then, too, there was a considerable amount of gas and flame leakage at the breech, and during the Civil War, at least one Confederate armory (Barrett) sealed the receivers, thereby making Hall breech loaders into muzzle loaders, and occasioning one Confederate to comment that this was "the best use which I have ever known Hall's carbines to be put to". (13) See page 157.

11002. CONFEDERATE ALTERED HALL'S RIFLE, made up from gun parts captured in 1862 by the Confederates at Harper's Ferry Arsenal, removed to Confederate Armories in Richmond, Va., or Fayetteville, N. C., where they were assembled into complete guns. Illustration shows plainly the Hall swinging block with brass plug and nipple screwed into the breech; the Hall safety hammer, guard bow, bands and other parts all assembled into a complete gun, which was used in service by the Confederates until captured by the Union troops near the close of the Civil War. Illustration is intended to show the breech mechanism. The barrel and stock is full length. The only breech loading gun on record, to our knowledge, which was altered back into muzzle loaders for army service.

The parts interchangeability is often a headache for collectors - - - many receivers are interchangeable - - - and the headache is not lessened by the fact that, for a number of years, Hall arms were also produced by contractor Simeon North.

- - - - - - - - - - - - - - - - - - - -

The principal feature of the Hall arms is the breech or "receiver". Hinged at the rear, it is raised by pulling backward and upward on the lever located forward of the trigger guard. The shooter bites the end off of a paper cartridge, pours the powder into the chamber of the receiver, pushes the ball in on top of the powder, and then pushes the receiver back into place.

After 1830, cartridge paper was made combustible by saturating it with nitre, and the need for biting was eliminated - - - the entire cartridge (powder, paper, ball and all) is placed into the chamber.

The external flintlock firing mechanism (cock, pan, etc.) on top of the receiver is offset to the right so as not to be in the line of sight, and the sights as well as the bayonet lug are offset to the left. This offsetting of sights and bayonet lug is not necessary on the percussion arms, and was not done on the Model 1840 Carbines. When flintlock receivers are placed in percussion arms that do not have offset sights, the line of sight is obscured by the firing mechanism.

The Hall arms are equipped with "hair triggers", i.e., the amount of trigger pull required to trip the hammer is adjustable by a screw that passes through the sear.

The bayonet and ramrod are finished bright, but all of the other non-moving parts such as the barrel and the iron furniture were first browned, and then coated with a clear lacquer.

Apparently, most Hall Harpers Ferry arms were browned, and apparently, the practice was continued even after the browning of muskets, etc., was discontinued in 1831. However, at least some rifles were finished bright - - - two specimens are at Rock Island, one with an 1824 dated receiver (No. R 243), and the other with an 1831 dated receiver (No. R 244).

The <u>Ordnance Manual</u> (1841) contains complete browning instructions, and this is, of course, a negative answer to Fuller's suggestion that the lacquer formula may have been destroyed when many of Harpers Ferry's buildings were burned in 1861. (14)

The iron moving parts (receiver, lever, lever plate, trigger, cock and frizzen, or hammer) are case hardened, and the heads of the screws are blued.

The pores of the wood are not filled, but the wood is polished with linseed oil.

Peterson indicates that Hall percussion receivers, removed from the arm, were sometimes carried and perhaps used as pistols. (15) The writer of this study has never fired a removed receiver, either percussion or flintlock; he has no intention of doing so; and he would not consider it wise for anyone else to do so.

Hall Rifle Model 1819.
(Maryland-Steuart).

The Hall Harpers Ferry Receivers

The receivers have bores of three different sizes:

.545 .69 .56

The .545 bore was intended for the Caliber .52 rifles (.525 ball, 32 to the pound), the .69 bore for the Caliber .64 smoothbore Model 1834 Carbines, and the .56 bore for the Caliber .52 smoothbore Model 1840 Carbines. Winant notes that a "bullet of slightly more than barrel bore diameter was used, so that gas from the powder explosion would not escape past the bullet and be wasted". (16)

Of course, it was (and is) not difficult to ream up a small bore to a larger bore.

Fuller gives additional receiver measurements (17) as follows:

Bore diameter	.545	.69	.56
Exterior diameter	1.	1.12	1.
Diameter of chamber	.1		.46
Depth of bore	1.1		1.4
Depth of chamber	1.3	2.48	.98

The writer of this study does not understand Fuller's "diameter of chamber" measurement of .1 on the receiver with the .545 bore.

Hicks, Plate 27, shows an 1837 dated rifle receiver with a bore of one uniform diameter, a chamber of a lesser uniform diameter, and a vent that runs straight downward from the pan to the chamber. Hicks, Plate 33, shows an 1839 dated carbine receiver with a bore-chamber shaped like a long, truncated cone, and with a vent that runs diagonally forward from the nipple to the bore-chamber.

The receivers have four types of markings:

Type A	Type B	Type C	Type D
J. H. Hall	J. H. Hall	J. H. Hall	H. Ferry
H. Ferry	U.S.	H. Ferry	U. S.
U. S.	18__	18__	18__
18__			

Hall was methodical, and it seems reasonable to conclude that the different type markings were meant to signify different things, and that he did not intend rifle receivers and carbine receivers to be interchanged.

The Type D marking gives no trouble. Apparently, it was used on all receivers made after Hall's death, i.e., on receivers made in years subsequent to 1840, and the reason for the omission of "J. H. Hall" is understandable.

The Type C marking is puzzling. The absence of "U.S." indicates that the receiver was not made for the Federal government, and, of course, Hall's "Rifle Works" was in some respects a semi-private enterprise.

The Type A and Type B markings also give trouble, and the following analysis is an attempt to define the sort of receivers upon which the several types of markings were used.

Rifles

I. Model 1819 - Caliber .52 (diameter of receiver bore .545)
II. Model 1841 - Caliber .52 (diameter of receiver bore .545)

A. Model 1819

Caliber .52 (diameter of receiver bore .545)

<u>Type A Marking</u> - most Model 1819 Harpers Ferry Rifle receivers have Type A markings.

<u>Type B Marking</u> - a few Model 1819 Harpers Ferry Rifle receivers have Type B markings. Examples: The 1837 dated receiver on Fuller Collection No. 460, and the 1837 dated specimen depicted in <u>Hicks</u>, Plate 27.

<u>Type C Marking</u> - a few Model 1819 Harpers Ferry Rifle receivers have Type C markings. Examples: The 1832 dated receivers on Fuller Collection No. 516, and the 1839 dated receiver on Fuller Collection No. 612.

B. Model 1841

<u>Type D Marking</u> - all Model 1841 Harpers Ferry Rifle receivers dated subsequent to 1840 have Type D markings (apparently no rifles were made in 1840).

Carbines

1. Model 1834 - Caliber .64 (diameter of receiver bore .69)
2. Model 1840 - Caliber .52 (diameter of receiver bore .56)

A. Model 1834

<u>Type A Marking</u> - apparently, most if not all Harpers Ferry receivers which are flintlock (or which appear to have been originally flintlock), and which are found on Model 1834 Carbines have Type A markings.

<u>Type B Marking</u> - apparently, most if not all of the Model 1834 Harpers Ferry Carbine receivers that were originally percussion have Type B markings.

B. Model 1840

<u>Type D Marking</u> - apparently, all Model 1840 Harpers Ferry Carbine receivers have Type D markings.

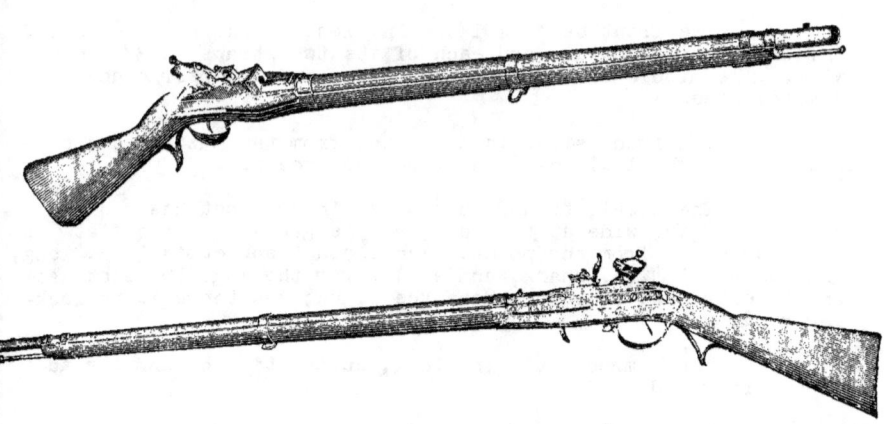

HALL'S BREECH-LOADING RIFLE,

The first arm of this class adopted by any Government. In actual service in the United States Army in 1825.

Model 1819 Rifle (Hall) (flintlock)

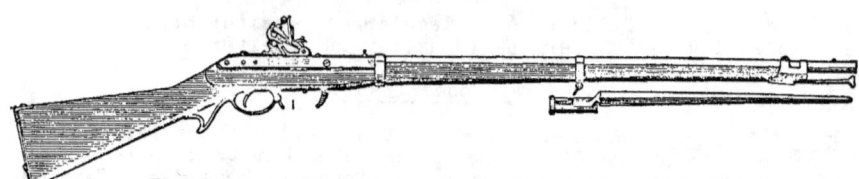

The Hall rifle has an overall length of 52 1/2 in., its weight without bayonet is 10 lbs. 4 oz., and its weight with bayonet is 10 lbs. 15 oz.

The stock is 49 1/2 in. long.

The 32 5/8 in. barrel is rifled with sixteen grooves (18), but to facilitate loading, the muzzle is smooth for the first 1 1/2 in.

Rifles made prior to 1831 have band springs; rifles made subsequent to 1831 have pin fastened bands; and some rifles made in 1831 have band springs, while others made in 1831 have pin fastened bands. (19) But according to Fuller, the pins preceded the springs - - - Fuller states that the pin fastened method was "extremely unhandy when dismounting the piece", and that "it was later changed to the band spring method". The writer believes that, in this respect, Fuller is in error.

The front band is 1 5/8 in. long at the top, and 2 1/2 in. long at the bottom, and each of its two straps is 3/8 in. wide. The middle band is 7/16 in. wide, and the rear band is 3/4 in. wide.

The front sight is 1 1/8 in. from the muzzle, and the open rear sight is 1 15/16 in. from the breech.

The steel, triangular 16 1/2 in. bayonet has a blade that is 7/8 in. wide at the base, and is grooved on the flat side for 9 in. from the point. The bayonet socket is 3 in. long, and has a 1 1/4 in. shank, and a slot for the lug; the slot has an offset recess to accommodate the sight; and there is no locking ring.

The ramrod is 32 in. long, button tipped, and threaded at the rear end.

Most rifles were finished brown, but some were finished bright. Examples: 1824 dated specimen at Rock Island (No. R 243), and 1831 dated specimen at Rock Island (No. R 244).

Hall flintlock rifles were made through 1839; apparently no Hall rifles were made in 1840; and after 1840, the Hall rifles were percussion. (20)

Model 1841 Rifle (Hall) (percussion)

In 1840, Hall went west to live with his son, and died at Moberly, Missouri, on February 26, 1841. (21)

In 1841, a new model Hall's rifle went into production at Harpers Ferry. It has a "fishtail" lever, a receiver that does not have a fence, a catch plate and a trigger guard plate that are one piece, a barrel that is rifled all the way to the muzzle (seven grooves), and a rear sling swivel attached to the rear of the trigger guard bow. Also, on the new model, the skeleton pistol grip is eliminated. (22)

Apparently, all of the hammers have holes bored through the throats.

- - - - - - - - - - - - - - - - - - -

Sing Sing

Lewis reports an account of the use of Hall rifles by guards at Sing Sing, and of the considerable number of shots that the guards were able to fire at escaping prisoners "before they got out of range". Lewis comments that the account is "a good plug for the rifles, but not for the guards' marksmanship". (22a)

Dragoon with Hall carbine.
1st Dragoons. 1847-1851.

Harpers Ferry Hall Carbines

Soldiers trained and equipped to fight on either horse or foot were needed on the United States' frontiers, and in 1833, the 1st Dragoon Regiment came into being.

The dragoon's long range firearm was the carbine - - - in 1833-4, Simeon North produced 1026 smoothbore percussion Caliber .58 Hall carbines for the 1st Dragoons. And in July of 1834, the Regiment left Fort Gibson on an expedition among the Indians living between the Mississippi River and the Rocky Mountains, each Dragoon being armed with a pistol, a sword and a Caliber .58 Hall-North carbine. (23)

Lewis points out that "a letter written in 1834 from the Ordnance Office to members of Congress who had been furnished Hall's carbines, referred users of these arms to local hardware stores for a supply of percussion caps, as the Army had none to issue". (24)

Model 1834 Carbine (Hall)

On September 3, 1836, Bomford wrote to Hall, directing that he "take the most energetic measures for the speediest manufacture" of 1000 carbines "carrying a ball weighing one eighteenth part of a pound", i.e., Caliber .69, "to be constructed with percussion locks". Of the 1000, a total of 715 were "required for the 2nd Regt. of Dragoons, which is now rapidly organizing". (25)

The production records show that Harpers Ferry made two model Hall carbines in 1836, and 1,017 Hall carbines in 1837, and the probabilities would seem to be that Harpers Ferry made what Bomford ordered, i.e., smoothbore percussion Caliber .69 carbines.

The 2nd Dragoons left for Florida (and the Second Seminole War) before the Hall Harpers Ferry carbines were ready, and rifled Caliber .52 carbines made by North were issued as substitutes. However, the Hall-North carbines proved faulty, and the 2nd Dragoons were then issued muzzle-loading flintlock muskets. But Hall Harpers Ferry carbines did see service in Florida before the War ended in 1842. (26)

Gluckman describes an 1837 dated flintlock specimen, and states that the carbines made at Harpers Ferry in 1837 were flintlock, but that "practically all were converted to percussion". Hicks, somewhat to the contrary, suggests that Hall, in order to save time in filling the 1000 carbine order, used parts originally intended for flintlock rifles, including such parts as stocks, trigger guards, and offset sights (27) The

Hall Carbines

Rod Bayonet. Flintlock. (Fuller No. 592).

Rod Bayonet. Percussion, patch box. (Fuller No. 631).

Ramrod. Fishtail lever. (Fuller No. 551).

Fishtail lever. (Lustyik).

Fuller Collection contains a specimen with an 1837 dated flintlock receiver (Fuller Collection No. 592), and another specimen with an 1838 dated flintlock receiver (Fuller Collection No. 652).

It is the belief of the writer of this study that Hall did not make any general issue flintlock carbines at Harpers Ferry, and that Hall flintlock receivers found on carbines are rifle receivers that have been altered or just interchanged. (28)

Fuller Collection No. 632 (receiver dated 1838) has a patch box as does Fuller Collection No. 631 (receiver dated 1839). There are no patch boxes on Fuller Collection No. 592 and No. 593, both of which have receivers dated 1837.

Apparently, all of the Model 1834 Carbines have offset sights, holes bored through the throats of the hammers, and bands that are pin fastened.

The Model 1834 Carbine has a 23 in. barrel, an overall length of 43 in., and an overall (with bayonet) length of 61 1/4 in. The rifle's skeleton pistol grip trigger guard extension is replaced by two small finger ridges on the lower trigger guard extension, and instead of sling swivels, the carbine has an eye bolt that passes horizontally through the grip of the stock. The carbine is equipped with a ramrod type bayonet, 21 1/2 in. long, and the carbine weighs 8.15 lbs. without the bayonet, and 8.40 lbs. with the bayonet. A portion of the pan (originally designed for the flintlock rifle), serves as a flash shield.

Some of the Model 1834 Carbines have "patch boxes" (for a combination tool and an extra nipple) opening from the bottom of the stock, and have hinged lids that form a prolongation of the trigger guard plates. Fuller states that patch boxes did not appear on Model 1834 Carbines until 1838. (29)

Model 1840 Carbine (Hall)

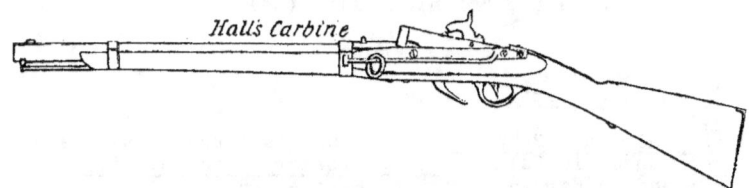

By letter dated January 8, 1842, Bomford wrote to Major Henry Knox Craig of Harpers Ferry, stating that "the Secretary of War directs that the utmost dispatch shall be used in making the carbines of the New Model * * * and you will send without delay a carbine of the New Model * * * that it may be put in the hands of the Contractor to work by". (30)

The Bomford production records show that 1001 carbines were made at Harpers Ferry in fiscal 1843.

Probably taking a cue from the Model 1841 "Mississippi" Rifle, the Model 1840 Hall Carbine is brass mounted, i.e., the butt plate, trigger guard bow, trigger guard plate, and bands are brass. It is Caliber .52 (reduced from Caliber .64), and it has a 21 in. smoothbore barrel. It also has a new type non-protruding lever (commonly called the "fishtail" lever) that was designed by Captain Benjamin Huger of Harpers Ferry, who later served with distinction as a Confederate general. (31) It has an overall length of 40 in. It has a 19 1/2 in. trumpet shaped ramrod (and no ramrod bayonet). Its weight without the bayonet is 7 lbs. It has neither finger ridges nor a hole in the throat of the hammer, and it has a bar and a sliding ring instead of an eye bolt.

It has a different type stock, and the receiver, originally designed for percussion, does not have a flash shield. Plate 36 of Hicks depicts an 1842 dated specimen.

Commodore Perry, preparing for his trip to Japan, requisitioned (April 19, 1852) forty-eight percussion Hall carbines, and forty-eight flintlock carbines, complete with bayonets. (32)

Rifled Carbines ?

Hicks mentions "rifle .52 Caliber carbines" that "appear to have been a special order for the State of Alabama", but apparently, these were made by North rather than by Hall. (33)

At the beginning of the Civil War, some of the Caliber .52 smoothbore carbines still on hand were rifled up to Caliber .58 to accomodate the "minnie ball". (34)

Notes

(1) American Rifleman June 1959, p. 20.
(2) Norton 11.
(3) Fairbairn and Patterson 8-9. Hall's patent drawings are reproduced in Fuller, Breech-Loader in the Service 19 and 23; and in Hardin, American Bayonet 25.
(4) American Rifleman June 1959, p. 20.
(5) Fairbairn and Patterson 9.
(6) Satterlee 54.
(7) See Note 7, Chapter III (Early Rifles).

(8)   Fuller and Steuart 67.
(9)   Norton 11.
(10) Fuller and Steuart 68. Fuller, Whitney Firearms
      136-145, et seq.
(11) Wasson, Hall Carbine Affair 60.
(12) Metschl
(13) Albaugh and Simmons, Confederate Arms 201.
(14) Fuller and Steuart 71.
(15) Peterson, Pageant of the Gun 122.
(16) Winant, Early Percussion Firearms 135.
(17) Fuller and Steuart 71-75. Measurements from the Fuller
      Collection Nos. 460, 592 and 551.
(18) The rifling is described in Fuller and Steuart 71-72.
(19) Fairbairn and Patterson 19.
(20) Ibid. 20.
(21) American Rifleman June 1959, p. 20.
(22) Hicks 69.
(22a) Letter to author. May 21, 1968.
(23) Gun Report Vol. XI, No. 4 (September 1965) p. 7.
(24) Lewis 56.
(25) Hicks 67.
(26) Huntington, "Hall Rifles at Harpers Ferry" p. 30 and 45.
(27) Gluckman 316; and Hicks 67.
(28) Lewis advises that all of the Harpers Ferry flintlock Hall
      carbines that he has seen have percussion type sights,
      but he calls attention to the fact that the Confederate
      Ordnance Manual notes Hall flintlock carbines as having
      been "formerly used".
(29) Fuller, Breech-Loader in the Service 47.
(30) Hicks 69.
(31) A photograph of a "fishtail" lever appears in Lustyik,
      Civil War Carbines 17.
(32) Gun Collector Vol. 33, p. 461.
(33) Russell 170.
(34) Lewis 56; and American Rifleman December 1955, p. 84.

86

Model 1840 Musket. Lockplate dated 1835. (Smithsonian).

VI. THE 1840 SERIES

During the 1830's there were many changes - - - changes from flintlock to percussion, changes necessitated by the introduction of new and better gunpowders, etc., and for Harpers Ferry, the 1840 Series was merely a prelude to the 1841-2 Series.

Model 1840 Musket (models and patterns)

In 1831, a Board of Officers was convened "with a view to the establishing of a uniform system in the operations of the Ordnance Department", and in 1833, a recommendation was made that the service muskets be like "the French musket manufactured at Mutzig in the year 1822", but with a round breech with two sides flattened (instead of an octagonal barrel), and the head of the ramrod was "to be of copper, to prevent battering the barrel". (1)

Apparently, a number of models were made at Harpers Ferry.

In 1838, the Military Storekeeper at the Washington Arsenal was ordered to send "eight muskets of the new model, and one set of verifying guages" to Springfield. Two of the muskets and the gauges were were intended for use at Springfield, and the other six were to be "carefully preserved subject to future orders". (2) The probabilities are that the eight muskets were made at Harpers Ferry.

By letter dated March 13, 1839, John Robb, the Superintendent at Springfield, advised Bomford that Springfield's Master Armorer (Thomas Warner) had been sent to Harpers Ferry where he would "by personal examination and conference with Mr. Moore make himself acquainted with the best method of proceeding with the manufacture of the tools". (Moore, according to Robb, had "found in the outset much difficulty in his operations, which would only be overcome by experimenting". (3)

It may well be inferred, from these references to difficulties, that the tools for the new weapons were to be of a type capable of turning out interchangeable parts.

By letter dated January 23, 1840, Bomford advised Robb that alterations were to be made in the "New Model" musket - - - "the change is now making at Harpers Ferry and you will be furnished with a correct Model (of 1840) as soon as practicable".

Lewis notes that "a manuscript Ordnance Regulation of 1839 refers to the 'New Model 1835 Musket'", but subsequent publications, including the Ordnance Manual (1841), calls the later, changed version "the Model of 1840". (4)

Changes made between 1835 and 1839, the date when the model was approved by the Ordnance Board, included eliminating the finger ridges from the trigger guard plate. The specimen depicted on Plate 30 of Hicks and the specimen in the Lewis Collection have finger ridges on the trigger guard plates, but there are no finger ridges on the Smithsonian specimen or on the specimen in the Fuller Collection (Fuller No. 843).

On all of these models, the lockplates and tangs are dated 1835, with the lockplates and all of the larger parts being marked "USM", while the small parts, such as the screws, are marked "M". The barrel of the Lewis specimen is marked "Model No. 16".

Lewis reports models (or patterns) that are marked like the models noted above except for 1840 dated lockplates.

And Lewis advises that, in addition to the finger ridges being eliminated, the models between 1835 and 1840 were changed by reducing the overall length from 58 in. to 57 1/2 in., reducing the barrel length from 42 3/4 in. to 42 in., increasing the length of the butt stock (measured to the breech) from 15 1/4 in. to 16 in., altering the guard bow swivel attachment from screw to rivet, and altering several screw sizes to reduce the number of different sizes used. (5)

The detachable brass pans are very large, they are horizontal, and each has a fence.

The frizzens are very wide. The bands are relatively narrow. And there is a comb in the butt stock.

Apparently no general issue Model 1840 Muskets were produced at Harpers Ferry - - - Harpers Ferry continued making the Model 1822 until at least 1843, and perhaps as late as 1844. (6)

Russell (quoting from The Ordnance Manual for the Use of Officers of the United States Army. Compiled by Maj. A. Mordecai, 2d ed. Charleston, S.C., 1861) gives this arm's dimensions and weight, comparing them with those of the Model 1822. (6a)

Model 1840 Musketoon (model and/or pattern)

In 1838, the Ordnance Board directed that Harpers Ferry make a model musketoon, (7) and the Fuller Collection includes an 1839 dated model or pattern. The production records show three pattern muskets made at Harpers Ferry in fiscal 1840, and these three may have been musketoons made in calendar 1839.

The Fuller specimen is Caliber .69, it is 41 in. overall (59 in. with bayonet); and it weighs 7 lbs. 3 oz. (without bayonet).

The lock (and all of the other large parts) are marked "USM", and all of the small parts, such as screws, are marked "M". The lockplate is 6 1/4 in. by 1 3/16 in.

Gluckman gives the measurement of the lockplate of a Harpers Ferry specimen as 5 1/2 in. by 1 1/4 in. (8)

The Fuller pan is brass. The rounded cock is 7/16 in. thick, and the round hole in the cock is 1/2 in. in diameter.

The stock is 38 in. long, and there is a 3/4 in. comb., 8 in. from the butt. The grip measures 1 3/4 in. by 1 1/2 in. The butt plate is 4 1/4 in. long, and is marked "US" on the tang.

The barrel, which has the usual "V", "P", and an eagle head markings, is 26 in. long. The bayonet stud on the bottom of the barrel is 2 in. from the muzzle. The breech tang is 2 in. long. The barrel is .84 in. in diameter at the muzzle, thus taking the standard 1840 bayonet. The blade front sight is brass.

All of the mountings are iron.

The trigger guard plate is 9 1/2 in. long.

Each of the two straps of the front band are 1/2 in. wide, the bottom of the band projects 1/2 in. to the rear; and the band's total length is 2 9/16 in. The front band spring is 2 3/4 in. long. The rear band is 5/8 in. wide on the top, and 1 in. wide at the bottom, and is retained by a 2 3/8 in. band spring forward of the band.

The front sling swivel is carried on a lug on the rear band, and has a sling opening of 1 3/8 in. The rear sling swivel is the same size, and is carried on a 2 1/2 in. plate at the butt of the stock.

The 25.7 in. ramrod is held in place by a spring or "spoon", and the rod channel has a metal stop.

Query: Were general issue musketoons produced at Harpers Ferry?

The Harpers Ferry production records do not show any musketoons as having been manufactured in either 1838, 1839 or 1840, but neither do those of Springfield. The Harpers Ferry production records show that one musketoon was made at Harpers Ferry in fiscal 1843. (9) The <u>Ordnance Manual</u> (1841) contains an illustration of a "Model 1840" musketoon, and the <u>Manual</u> indicates that the regular bayonet could be used.

<u>Hicks</u>, Plate 34, a drawing of the Springfield Armory Museum specimen, does not show a bayonet lug, but an accompanying sketch (on Plate 34) shows a barrel with a bayonet lug.

Chapel cautions "beware of fakes". (10)

Lewis advises that the "search for a new musketoon kept along for several years", and that in 1842, both of the national armories produced models of suggested flintlock musketoons. Lewis' collection includes one of the Harpers Ferry models, lockplate dated 1842, that follows "the Model 1822 configuration, that Model still being the tooling available there". He reports that "the stock is special (not possible to cut down from a musket stock)", and that the distance from the breech to the bottom of the rear band is 11 1/2 in. (as opposed to 11 1/4 in. on the Model 1822 Musket), and that the distance from the breech to the bottom of the front band is 27 1/2 in. (as opposed to 25 in., the distance to the corresponding middle band on the Model 1822 Musket). The stock is stamped "JAS". Most of the parts are marked "11", but the rear sight is marked "16", as is the barrel (behind the rear sight), and these "16" marks may concern the sight only. The barrel is Caliber .69, had shallow rifling, and at the muzzle, its diameter is .84 in. (11)

This musketoon may have been the musketoon shown on the production records as having been made at Harpers Ferry in fiscal 1843.

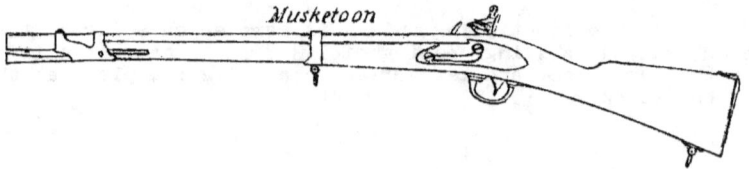

91

Notes

(1) Hicks 64.
(2) Ibid. 65.
(3) Ibid. 66.
(4) Memorandum to author. May 1968.
(5) Lewis 48.
(6) Fuller, Whitney Firearms 192; and Patterson 29.
(6a) Russell 324.
(7) Hicks 68.
(8) Gluckman 306.
(9) Ibid. 307.
(10) Chapel, Gun Collector's Handbook of Values 243.

Model 1840 Musket.
Lockplate dated
1835. (Smithsonian).

"Mississippi". Lockplate dated 1848. (Smithsonian).

"Mississippi". Lockplate dated 1851. (Bovee).

VII. THE 1841-1842 SERIES (percussion)

Commencing in about 1840, and no doubt encouraged by Captain Hall's successes, the United States instituted a practical program of producing arms with interchangeable parts. A model rifle made at Harpers Ferry was approved in 1841, and a model musket made at Springfield was approved in 1842. (1) The probabilities are that the production of regular issue arms did not begin at Harpers Ferry until 1844. (2)

The buildings and machinery of Hall's Rifle Works were converted, and then used in the production of the Model 1841 Rifle. (3)

In 1851, the products of the two national armories were tested for parts interchangeability with one Model 1842 Musket being taken from each armory, and the only appreciable variation found was in the front end of the lockplate. Then, in 1852, there came the pudding-poof at Harpers Ferry when the "highest flood ever known at the place" submerged some 20,000 stands of arms. Some 9,000 Model 1842 muskets inclued in the submerged 20,000 were "completely dismantled, their parts being thrown into great masses", and after the parts were cleaned and dried, 9,000 muskets were put together from the parts. (4)

Model 1841 Rifle

"Mississippi"

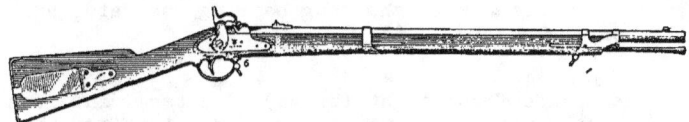

This rifle served effectively in 1847 at Buena Vista with the 1st Mississippi Regiment commanded by Colonel Jefferson Davis, and "when the war was over the soldiers were so pleased with their guns that they agreed to retain them, the War Department deducting the costs (about $14.00) from their pay - - - this gave rise to the name "Mississippi". (5) The Confederates officially labelled it the "Mississippi" (6), and it was also called the "Windsor", the "Kentucky", the "Harpers Ferry", and the "Yaeger" - - - and in Virginia, the latter word was pronounced "Yawger".

It was a splendid military weapon - - - Sawyer classifies it as "the best made and most accurate spherical bullet military rifle in the world". (7)

It also served non-military purposes - - - Sawyer notes that "a surprising number of duels were fought by civilians with Model 1841 rifles in the period from 1850 to 1865" (8), and Lord states that "big game hunters swore by it". (9)

The rifle caliber (.54) remains the same, but "in recognition of the fearful kick of our former military rifles", the Model 1841 "used a reduced powder charge for the old style half-ounce ball". (10)

The arm has an overall length of 48 1/2 in., it weighs 9 lbs. 12 oz.

The lockplate measures 5 1/4 in. by 1 1/4 in.

The 43 1/2 in. stock has a 3/4 in. comb, and inspector's initials, such as "JK", "JLR", etc., are stamped on the stock on the side opposite the lock. The patch box (brass) measures 7 5/8 in. by 1 11/16 in., and has a spring hinge.

Lewis' collection includes a pattern piece and a set of inspection guages. The barrel is marked "Harpers Ferry 1841 Model No. 1", and all other parts are marked "USM" or "M". The barrel is 33 1/16 in. long; the arm's overall length is 48 1/2 in.; there is no bayonet lug; and the front band is like that of the Model 1840 Musket. (10a)

On the regular issue Model 1841 Rifle, the barrel markings are the same type as those on the Model 1819 Pistol (pattern), plus inspector's initials. The tang is dated, and specimens are reported with the tang bearing one date, and the lockplate bearing another. (11)

The blade front sight (brass), located 1 in. from the muzzle, and the V-notch rear sight, located 3 in. from the breech, are set for 50 yds.

The rifle as originally designed did not have a bayonet.

The 9 in. trigger guard plate, the bow, the side plate, and the butt plate are brass.

The bands also are brass. The front band is 3 3/8 in. long (each of its two straps is 1/2 in. wide), and the rear band is 11/32 in. wide at the top, and 1 1/16 in. wide at the bottom. The band springs are steel.

The trigger bow ends are threaded, and are fastened to the trigger guard plate by round slotted nuts.

The butt plate measures 4 3/8 in. by 1 3/4 in.

The steel ramrod has a brass tip that is cupped at the front end. The rear end is threaded, and is held in place by a spoon.

Sawyer describes the barrel as being "acid browned"; the trigger, screw heads and band springs as being "heat blued"; the exterior lock parts as being "case hardened gray with faint mottled colors"; the ramrod and sling swivels as being "bright polished"; the brass furniture as being "polished"; and the wood as being "dull, oil finished". (12)

Alterations

Contemporaneous with the adoption of the "minnie ball", Secretary of War Jefferson Davis, on July 5, 1855, approved an Ordnance Board directive that the Model 1841 Rifle be re-rifled to Caliber .58. Also, because the ballistics of the "minnie ball" differed from the rifle ball, the arm was ordered equipped with a longer range sight.

And, thirdly, the arm was to be equipped with a bayonet lug, and a sword bayonet. (13)

The long range rear sight was either the fully adjustable, adjusting screw, folding leaf sight, or the two leaf type that was used on the later Model 1855 Rifles and Rifle Muskets.

There were two types of sword bayonets: a stud type and a ring type. The stud type fastens either (1) to a stud welded to the right side of the barrel just to the rear of the muzzle, an alteration that necessitated the shortening of the stock, and the replacement of the front band with a shorter band in order to make room for the hilt of the sword bayonet; or (2) to a stud that is a part of a split, 9/16 in. wide ring band that is locked to the barrel by means of a tightening screw. The ring type bayonet has a ring on the top of its handle that fits over the barrel, and the bayonet also has a locking bar that fits into a horizontal notch cut into the right side of the muzzle, and that fits into a vertical groove cut into the barrel a short distance to the rear of the notch. (14)

One sword bayonet is described as having a brass mounted leather scabbard and frog that measures 26 1/2 in. overall. (15) The bayonet's blade is 21 3/4 in., it has a brass hilt 4 3/4 in., and it weighs 2 lbs. 10 oz. With the scabbard and the frog, the bayonet weighs 2 lbs. 14 oz. In 1855 and 1856, the Harpers Ferry musket works manufactured sword bayonets for the Mississippi rifles. (16)

Model 1842 Musket. Lockplate dated 1844. (Fuller No. 599).

Hicks, Plate 38, shows the two types of long range rear sights, the two types of bayonets, the three types of barrel attachments, and the shorter front band. Attachment drawings are also shown on page 7 of Webster's article, "The Mississippi Rifle".

A drawing by Robert Miller "U.S. Waist Belt for Sword Bayonets c. 1855-1865" appears in Lord's article, "The Mississippi Rifle".

After 1859, a musket type front sight on a square post was added to rifles that had not previously been altered for bayonets, and the regular socket type triangular musket bayonet was used. (17)

Also, the barrels on some Model 1841 Rifles were turned down at the muzzle to take the regular triangular bayonet. (18)

After 1858, probably in 1859, a number of the Model 1841 Rifles were converted to breech loaders by the Lindner, the Merrill, the Miller, and other systems. (19)

The Mississippi was used in the Indian Campaigns by such regular army units as the 4th Infantry. "The soldier of that day believed that with this rifle he could hit an Indian nearly every time at ranges up to 1000 yards". (20)

Model 1842 Musket

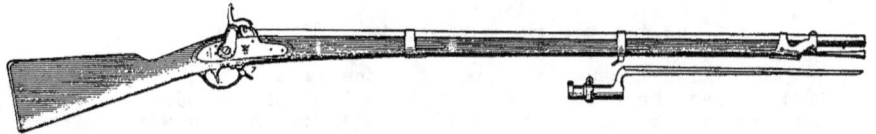

The earliest specimen of which the writer of this study has knowledge has an 1844 dated lockplate, and an 1843 dated barrel tang. (21)

The Model 1842 Musket was to be "arranged on the same principle" as the Model 1841 Rifle, and is virtually the same as the Model 1840 Musket (except, of course, the Model 1840 is flintlock).

The musket caliber (.69) is retained, as is the 42 in. barrel. The overall length is 57 3/4 in., and the arm weighs 9 3/4 lbs.

The lockplate is 6 1/4 in. by 1 1/4 in.

The stock is 55 in. long.

The barrel is marked with the same type of markings as the Model 1819 Pistol (pattern), and the 2 in. tang is dated. There is a bayonet lug on the bottom of the barrel 1 1/2 in. from the muzzle.

The bands are iron, the front band being 3 in. long, with a 9/16 in. front strap that carries the blade front sight (brass), and a 1/2 in. rear strap. The middle band is 9/16 in. long, and the rear band is 9/16 in. long at the top, and 1 1/16 in. long at the bottom. Apparently, the front sights on most specimens are brass, but iron front sights are known. (22)

The iron trigger guard plate is 9 5/8 in. long, and the iron trigger guard bow is held to the plate by two round, threaded nuts. The trigger is hung on an inside trigger guard plate stud.

The iron butt plate is 4 1/2 in. long, and is marked "US" on the tang.

The 42 1/2 in. steel ramrod has an elongated, trumpet-shaped head, and seats against an iron stop at the bottom of the ramrod channel where it is held in place by a spring.

The arm was finished bright although a Flayderman catalogue lists an 1848 dated specimen that is finished brown - - - "only browned specimen we have ever viewed". (23)

The trigger guard plate is 9.625 in.

The arm was equipped for the triangular, clamping band 18 in. blade bayonet (marked "U.S.") that has a 2 5/8 in. socket, and weighs 5/8 lbs. The overall length of the arm with bayonet is 75.8 in.

In 1854, or thereabouts, many of the 1842 Muskets were rifled to take the "minnie ball", and at this time, since these arms would henceforth be aimed at, rather than just pointed at a target, some were equipped with a large, long range, "sidewall" rear sight of the type with which the Model 1855 Rifle Muskets were equipped up until 1858. This sight is larger than the long range sight used on the Mississippi. <u>Hicks,</u> Plate 39, includes a drawing of this sight.

The Model 1842 Musket was used to some extent during the Mexican War, and to a great extent during the early years of the Civil War.

It was superseded by the Model 1855 Rifle Musket.

Musketoon

By letter dated June 4, 1844, the Ordnance Office advised Springfield that "the Model Musketoon and Model Dragoon Carbines as now adjusted, have been addressed to you from the Harpers Ferry Armory". (24) The musketoon may have been the musketoon shown on the production records as having been made at Harpers Ferry in fiscal 1843.

Crocker states that a number of Model 1842 Muskets were made in shorter lengths - - - "probably made up from barrels, otherwise perfectly good, which were rejected for defects near the muzzle". (25)

A dealer lists a Harpers Ferry Model 1842 Musket with three bands, and an original 32 in. barrel - - - "made this way at the arsenal". (26)

Another dealer catalogues a "Harpers Ferry rifled musketoon, dated 1850, with the Merrill breech loading alteration. Brass patch box, brass trigger guards and bands, Cal. 58". (27)

Notes

(1) Hicks 70; and Crocker, "U. S. Model 1842 Musket".
(2) Cartridge 28-9.
(3) Fairbairn and Patterson 18.
(4) Fuller and Steuart 34.
(5) Bannerman Catalogue 1949, p. 27. Lord, "The Mississippi Rifle" p. 37, states that Jefferson Davis' 1st Mississippians used rifles made by Whitney.
(6) Lewis 49.
(7) Sawyer 141.
(8) Ibid. 142.
(9) Lord, "The Mississippi Rifle"
(10) Russell 190; and Sawyer 141.
(10a) Letter to author. May 21, 1968. Sawyer, describing a pattern Model 1841 Rifle, states that the bore has seven grooves "almost semi-circular at breech, segmental at the muzzle, about two-thirds the width of the lands"; that the grooves make one turn in six feet; and that the grooves are .005 in. deep at the muzzle, and .013 in. deep at the breech.
(11) Patterson and Rich.
(12) Sawyer 143.
(13) Ibid. 150.
(14) Patterson and Rich 6.
(15) Ibid.
(16) Davis, U. S. Sword Bayonets 7.
(17) Webster, "The Mississippi Rifle" p. 7; and Fuller and Steuart 37-8.

(18) Gluckman 182.
(19) Sawyer 145; and Cartridge No. 226.
(20) Lord, "The Mississippi Rifle" p. 36.
(21) Gun Report Vol. III, No. 12 (May 1958) p. 27.
(22) Patterson and Rich 6.
(23) Flayderman Catalogue 79, Item 719.
(24) Hicks 73.
(25) Crocker, "U. S. Model 1842 Musket" p. 26.
(26) Eric Vaule. Advertisement in Gun Report Vol. XI, No. 7 (December 1965) p. 67.
(27) Kimball Catalogue 6, p. 15.

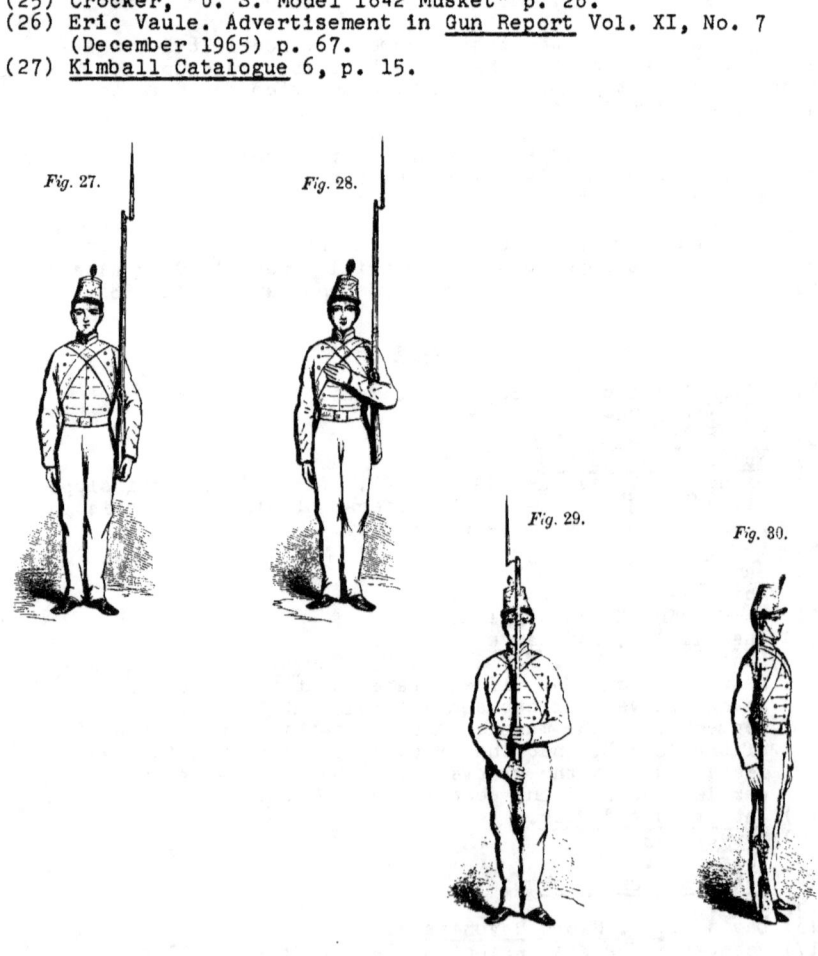

Fig. 27.   Fig. 28.   Fig. 29.   Fig. 30.

VIII. THE 1855 SERIES

In 1853, Harpers Ferry's James Henry Burton developed a conical bullet that was a modification of a projectile designed by Capt. C. E. Minié of the French Army. Burton's bullet was and is called a "minnie ball", but, of course, it is not a ball.

In 1853, Harpers Ferry manufactured a test batch of 5,000 "minnie ball" cartridges, and in 1855, following several years of experimenting, the Ordnance Office decided that all United States small arms would use Burton's speedy loading, deadly accurate, deeply penetrating "minnie ball".

BALLS FOR NEW RIFLE-MUSKET AND PISTOL-CARBINE.

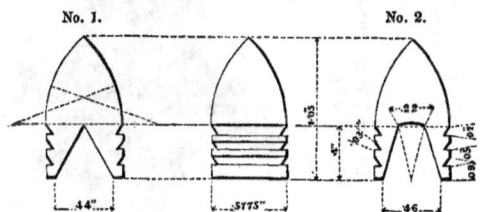

Weight of No. 1, 500 grains. Weight of No. 2, 450 grains.
Weight of powder, 60 grains. Weight of powder, 40 grains.
No. 1, section of musket ball.
No. 2, section of pistol-carbine ball.
Both balls have the same exterior.

To effectively accomodate the "minnie ball" (Caliber .58), all small arms were to have the three groove, Enfield type bores, with each groove being .3 in. wide, and with the grooves of the rifle and of the rifle musket making one turn in six feet, and the grooves of the pistol-carbine making one turn in four feet. The "minnie ball" used in the pistol-carbine is lighter in weight than that used in the rifle and rifle musket.

Also, in 1855, the Ordnance Office decided that all small arms would be equipped with the Maynard primer, with the locks of the rifle and of the rifle musket being designed for tapes having twenty-five primers.

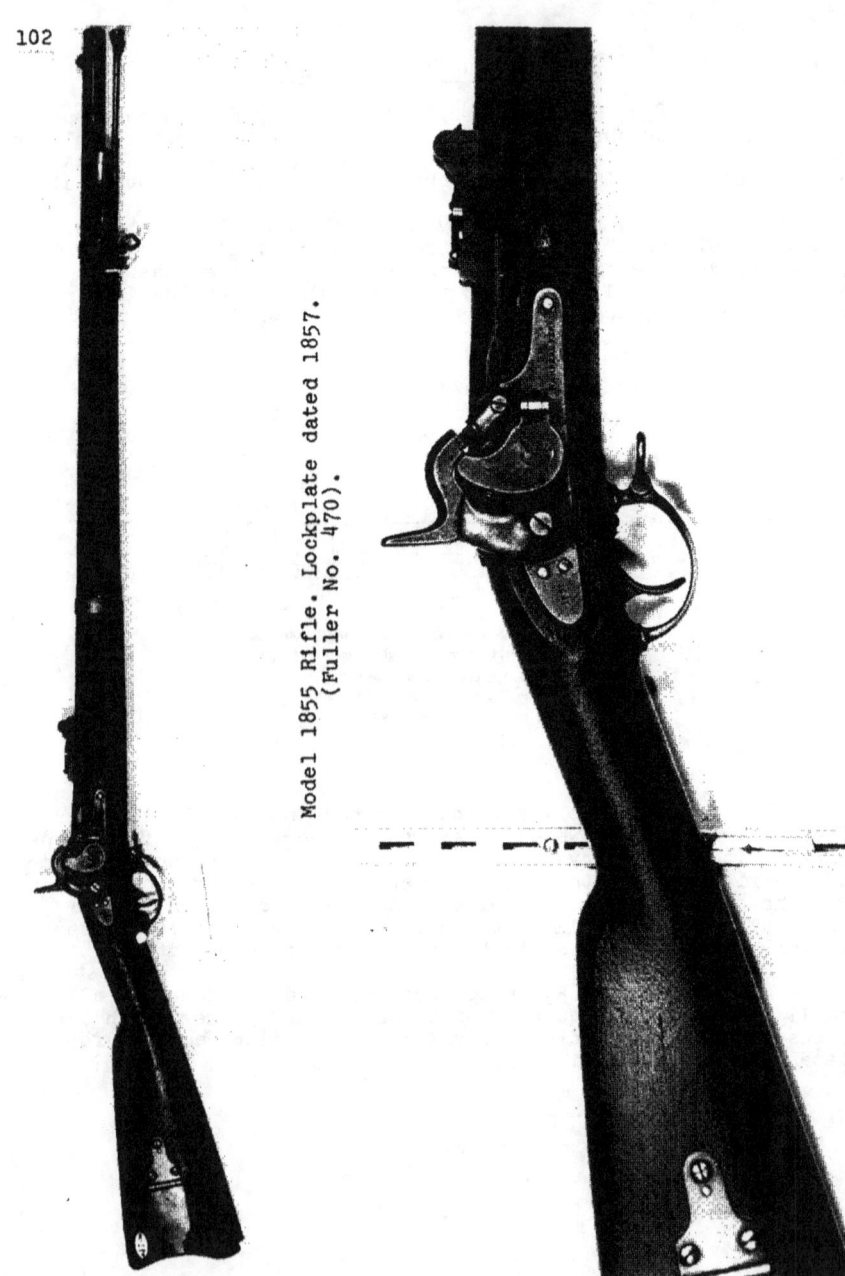

Model 1855 Rifle. Lockplate dated 1857. (Fuller No. 470).

103

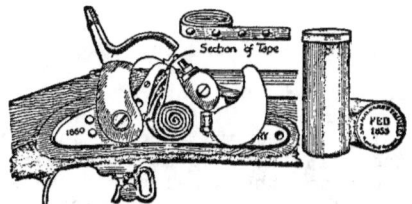

MAYNARD TAPE PRIMERS. Made for use in Civil War army muskets. Tape containing 50 charges of fulminate, was inserted in the lock, and each time the hammer was pulled back the feed finger spring mechanism pushed a section of the tape containing cap over the nipple, the hammer in descending simultaneously cut off the tape and exploded the cap,

These tapes gave the soldier a double chance. He could use either tape or percussion cap.

Finally, the percussion cone would have a removable screw in its side, making it possible to clean out the passage leading from the cone to the barrel.

The stocks were coated with linseed oil, but were not polished. (1)

Model 1855 Rifle

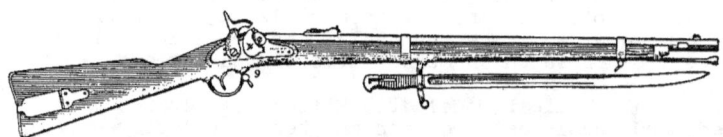

Under date of July 5, 1855, in approving the 1855 Series, Secretary of War Jefferson Davis stated that "the present rifle (the Model 1841 Rifle), modified by the adoption of the new caliber and primer lock, will be continued and will be issued to the sappers instead of the sappers' musketoon, the manufacture of which will be discontinued". (2)

Apparently, the Model 1855 Rifle was first regularly produced at Harpers Ferry in 1856, (3) and it was produced only at Harpers Ferry. (4) However, Springfield 1855 Series locks are interchangeable with Harpers Ferry 1855 Series locks, and Model 1855 Rifles with Springfield locks have been reported.

The caliber is .58.

The overall length is 49.3 in., and with the bayonet, 72 in. The weight is 9.93 lbs. without the bayonet, and 13 lbs. complete with the bayonet.

The lockplate is 5 1/2 in. by 1 7/8 in.

The stock is 44 in. long.

The 33 in. barrel has grooves that are .005 in. deep at the muzzle, and .015 in. deep at the breech. (5) The barrel is dated, and otherwise, the usual barrel markings are the same as those on the Model 1819 Pistol (pattern). A specimen with a barrel date differing from the lockplate date are not uncommon. There is a stud on the right side of the barrel for a sword bayonet.

The trigger guard bow is secured to the 7 1/2 in. trigger guard plate by two threaded, round nuts.

The 33 in. ramrod is cup-tipped, and has a swelling near its forecap that fits into a recess inside the stock, thus holding the ramrod in place.

The spring hinged patch box is smaller than that on the Model 1841 Rifle, and was used for grease and accessories rather than for patches - - - the "minnie ball" did not require a patch.

The Model 1855 Rifle has two bands, the wide front band of the Model 1841 Rifle having been replaced by a narrow front band and an end cap. The end cap of the Model 1855 Rifle differs in shape from those on the other arms of the series.

The earliest Model 1855 Rifles (ca. 1856-58) are brass mounted, and the latest are iron mounted. By letter dated April 21, 1859, the Ordnance Office ordered Springfield to substitute "malleable iron for the tips of rifle and musket stocks, instead of brass", and ordered that the patch box covers were to be "blued iron" instead of brass. (6) The probabilities seem to be that Harpers Ferry received similar orders.

The brass end cap is riveted to the stock whereas the iron end cap is attached to the stock by means of a screw.

On the early rifles, the patch box is inletted so as to contain an extra nipple, and a figure eight front sight with cross wires, (7) but the Ordnance Office's letter of April 21, 1859, directed that "the cavity under the patch box cover * * * be cleared of projecting wood and enlarged to the greatest capacity the cover will admit of". (8) The separate cross wire sight could be mounted on the barrel in front of the regular front sight, and was held in place by a knurled set screw. (9)

At least some of the earlier rifles were finished "brown" (10) - - - Sawyer states that these were "issued for a trial", and that the varnish used was made in the proportion of one fifth ounce of dragon's blood, and one ounce of shellac dissolved in one quart of alcohol. (11) The other Model 1855 Rifles were finished "bright". The lock, patch box cover and buttplate are case hardened. The bands are blued.

On the earlier Model 1855 Rifles, there is a large, long range, high "sidewall" rear sight adjustable to nine different elevations, the side plate being graduated to 500 yards. (12) On later Model 1855 Rifles, there is the smaller two leaf rear sight, the base having a notch graduated for 100 yards, and the two leaves that fold down onto the base having ranges, respectively, of 300 and 500 yards. (13)

The probabilities seem to be that the five changes (brass mountings to iron mountings, brass end cap to iron end cap, inletted patch box cavity to fully cleared patch box cavity, "brown" finish to "bright" finish, and large rear sight to small rear sight) were made ca. 1859, and that all were made at the same time or at approximately the same time.

Patterson states that the changes from brass mountings and brass end cap to iron mountings and iron end cap took place in two steps: first, all of the mountings including the patch box but excepting the end cap were changed to iron, and, second, the brass end cap was changed to iron. (14)

The brass-handled, brass-hilted sword bayonet measures 26 1/2 in. overall, has a 21 3/4 in. blade, and weighs 2 lbs. 2 oz. (15)

Between 1857 and 1860, Harpers Ferry made 9721 sword bayonets. (16)

When Harpers Ferry was burned on April 18, 1861, the Rifle Works were not destroyed, and production was continued during the approximately two months that Harpers Ferry was in the hands of the Virginia Militia. But, apparently, Harpers Ferry made only rifle muskets during this period.

A Model 1855 Rifle, made at Harpers Ferry for Secretary of War John D. Floyd, was used exclusively by him in target practice. (17)

A late specimen has both lockplate and barrel dated 1861. (18)

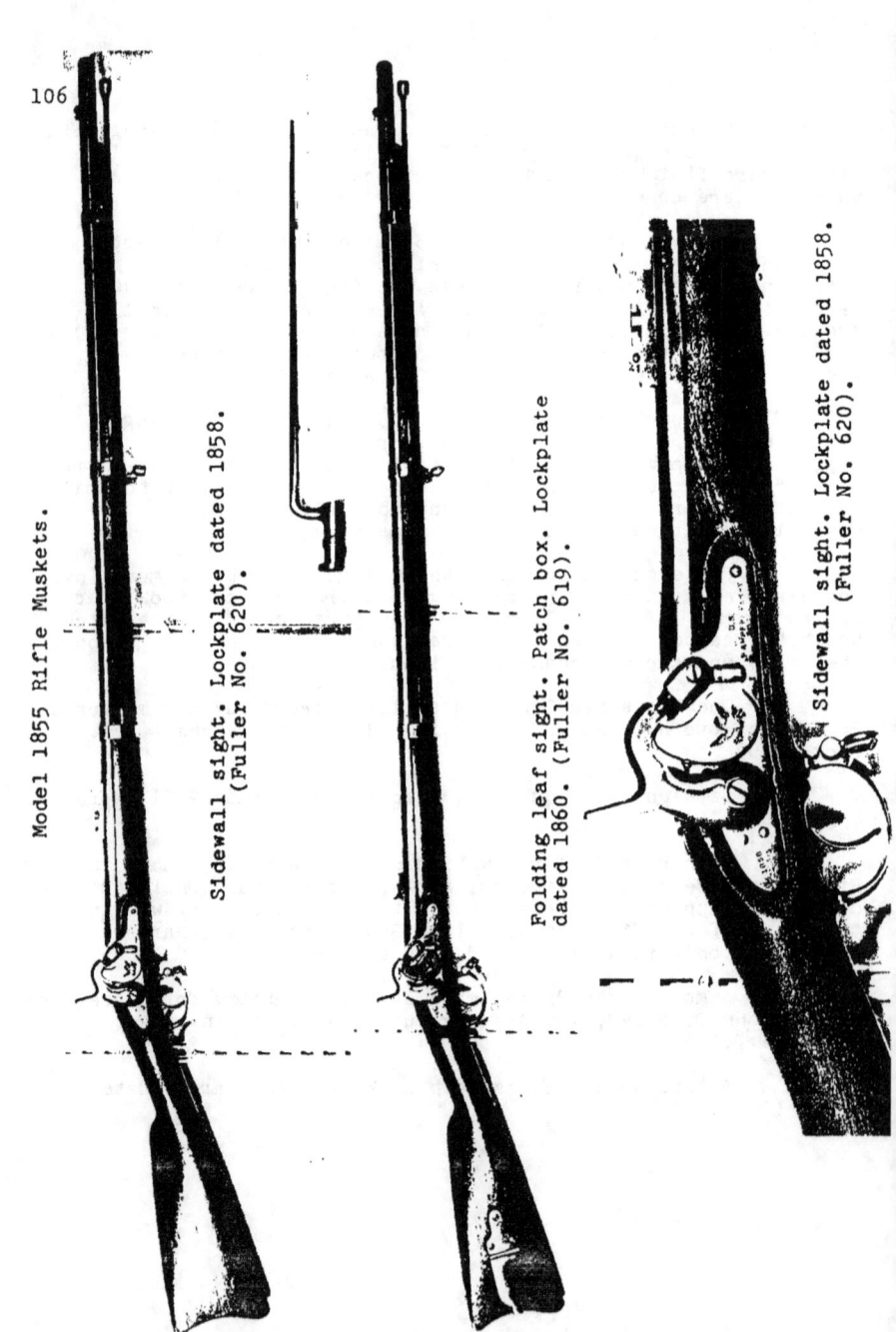

Model 1855 Rifle Muskets.

Sidewall sight. Lockplate dated 1858. (Fuller No. 620).

Folding leaf sight. Patch box. Lockplate dated 1860. (Fuller No. 619).

Sidewall sight. Lockplate dated 1858. (Fuller No. 620).

Model 1855 Rifle Musket

The Model 1855 Rifle Musket, which went into production at Harpers Ferry in 1856 or 1857, (19) is similar to and just as much a <u>rifle</u> as is the Model 1855 Rifle - - - it is called a musket only because of its size. The caliber (.58), rifling, bullet and powder charge are the same as those of the Model 1855 Rifle, but there is a difference in the barrel length, i.e., 40 in. for the rifle musket as compared with 33 in. for the rifle. Also the barrel of the rifle musket is not as heavily constructed as that of the rifle. And the rifle musket has three bands instead of two.

The rifle musket has an overall length of 58 1/2 in. (74 in. with the regular triangular bayonet), and it weighs 9.25 lbs. without the bayonet, and 9.90 lbs. with the bayonet.

The early rifle muskets did not have patch boxes, (20) but the Ordnance Office's letter of April 21, 1859, directed that the rifle musket thenceforth have an iron "grease or patch box" like the rifle, and that "the cavity under the patch box cover", like that of the rifle "be cleared of projecting wood and enlarged to the greatest capacity the cover will admit of". (21)

The early rifle muskets (1857-58) have the large, long range, "sidewall" rear sight located six inches from the breech. This sight is like that found on the early Model 1855 Rifle except that the side plate is graduated up to 400 yards, instead of being graduated up to 500 yards (as is that on the Model 1855 Rifle). (22) The later rifle muskets have the smaller two leaf rear sight (like that found on the later Model 1855 Rifles) located 3 in. from the breech.

Also, the brass end caps of the early rifle muskets were changed to iron pursuant to the order of the Ordnance Office contained in its letter of April 21, 1859.

As regards the three changes (no patch box to patch box, large rear sight to small rear sight, and brass end cap to iron end cap), the probabilities seem to be that all were made in 1859, and that all were made at the same time. However, in using up parts on hand, overlaps may have resulted.

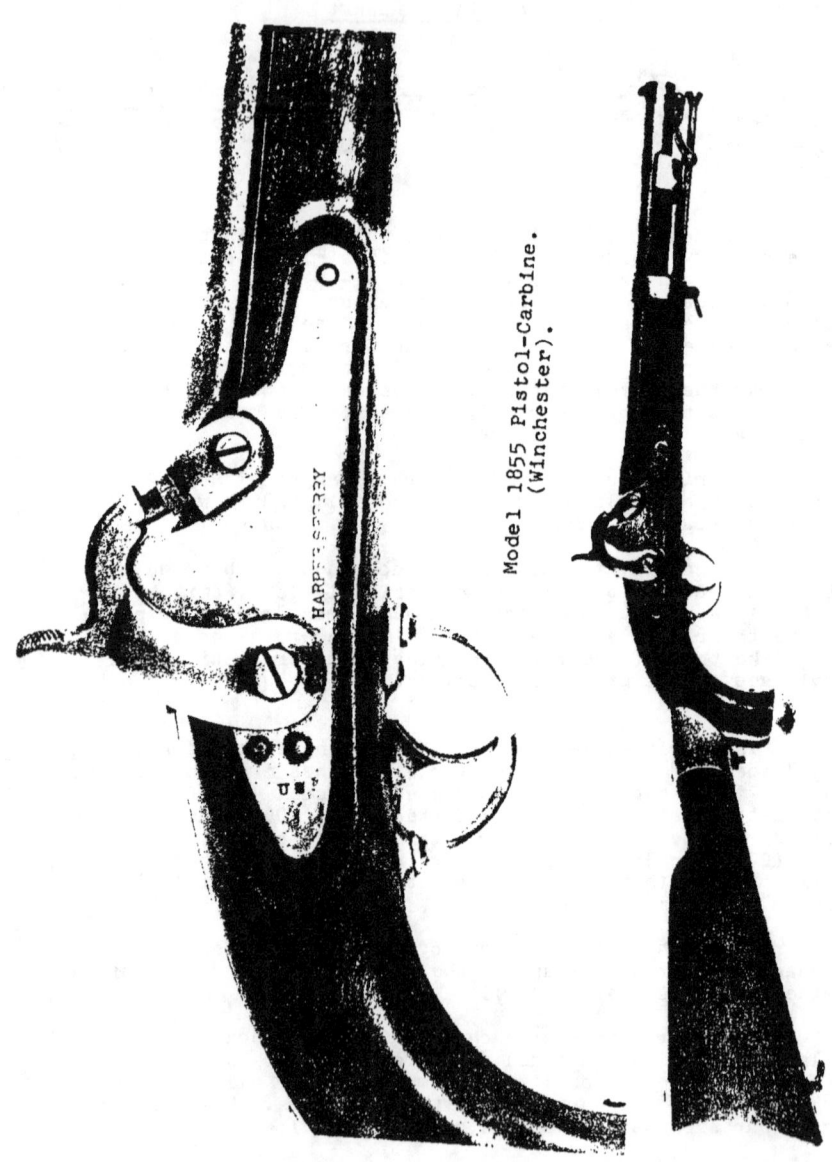

Model 1855 Pistol-Carbine. (Winchester).

Rifle muskets were made at Harpers Ferry during at least some of the period between April 18, 1861, the date of its partial burning and total evacuation by the Union garrison (and of its capture by the Virginia Militia), and June 18, 1861, the date of its evacuation by the Virginia Militia.

Shortly after April 18, 1861, Virginia's "Stonewall" Jackson reported to Virginia's Robert E. Lee that "Mr. Burkhart, who is in charge of the rifle-factory, reports that he can furnish fifteen hundred rifle-muskets in thirty days", and by letter dated April 22, 1861, Gen. Kenton Harper of the Virginia Militia reported that the rifle factory was "turning out daily several hundred minie muskets". (23)

Any Harpers Ferry rifle musket dated 1861 might be either U.S. or C.S.A. (Virginia Militia).

While Harpers Ferry was under the control of the Virginia Militia, many incompletely made, tested or marked parts may well have been used in the "daily" production of the "several hundred minie muskets" - - - the Maryland-Steuart Collection No. 78 with an 1861 dated Harpers Ferry lockplate, a brass end cap, a small rear sight, and a Maynard primer, but with no barrel markings is probably an example.

Model 1855 Pistol-Carbine

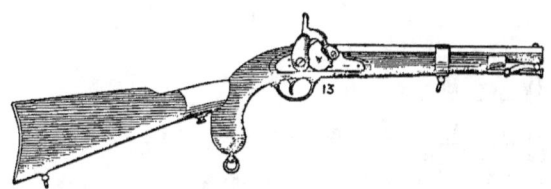

Secretary of War Jefferson Davis, in his letter of July 5, 1855, directed that "the pistol will be provided with a removable stock, by the application of which it may be used as a carbine for light artillery and mounted troops". (24)

A dealer's catalogue lists a "U.S. Martial Harpers Ferry Model 1855 Pistol-Carbine * * * Maynard tape primer". (25)

Harpers Ferry, in its 1857-8 budget estimate, requested machinery to manufacture the pistol-carbine. (26)

The undated model or pattern pictured herein (page 108) has an overall length of 17 3/4 in. The overall length of the detachable brass-mounted shoulder stock is 11 1/4 in., and the overall length of the pistol with stock affixed is 28 1/4 in.

    The lockplate (designed for the Maynard primer) has not been milled for the Maynard primer, and the blade on the hammer has been filed down (there being no need to cut off paper behind an exploded Maynard cap).

    The 12 in. barrel, semi-octagonal at the breech, has the same markings as does the Model 1819 Pistol (pattern).

    The steel blade front sight is brazed to the barrel. There is no rear sight.

    Apparently, the pistol-carbine was designed at Harpers Ferry, but apparently, only a very few, if any, regular issue pistol-carbines were produced at Harpers Ferry.

    Van Rensselear reports Harpers Ferry pistol-carbines equipped with Maynard primers, and "dated 1850 or 1857". (27)

Model 1855 Rifle Carbine (?)

    Chapel intimates that Model 1855 Rifle Carbines were made by both of the national armories. (28)

Notes

(1) Sawyer 149.
(2) Fuller, Rifled Musket 5.
(3) Patterson 3.
(4) Fuller, Rifled Musket 10.
(5) Sawyer 149.
(6) Fuller, Rifled Musket 8 and 10.
(7) Metschl 121-122 (N3499).
(8) Hicks 84; and Fuller, Rifled Musket 8.
(9) Hicks, Plate 46.
(10) Fuller, Rifled Musket 10.
(11) Sawyer 149.
(12) Gun Report Vol. VI, No. 10 (March 1961) p. 4.
(13) Fuller, Rifled Musket 29.
(14) Patterson 14.
(15) Gun Report Vol. VII, No. 5 (October 1961) p. 7; and Patterson and Rich 7.
(16) Davis, U. S. Sword Bayonets 13.
(17) Sawyer MSS Notes.
(18) Gun Report Vol. VII, No. 5 (October 1961) p. 7.
(19) Patterson 29. See Gluckman 227-228.
(20) Patterson 30.
(21) Fuller, Rifled Musket 8.

(22) Gun Report Vol. VI, No. 10 (March 1961) p. 4.
(23) Fuller and Steuart 56-57.
(24) Fuller, Rifled Musket 5.
(25) Museum of Historical Arms Catalogue 15 (1963), Item 11777.
(26) Gurney 44; and "Annual Production Data, Arms and Tools and Expenditures at the United States Armory at Harper's Ferry, Va., 1796-1860".
(27) Van Rensselear 112.
(28) Chapel, Guns of the Old West 66.

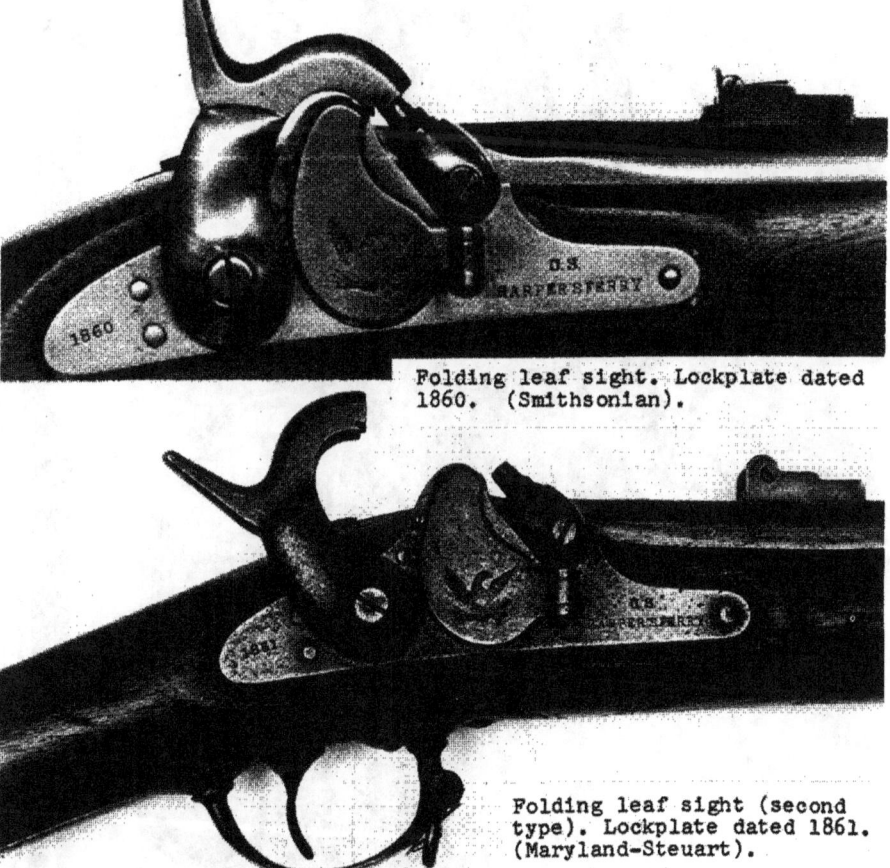

Model 1855 Rifle Muskets.

Folding leaf sight. Lockplate dated 1860. (Smithsonian).

Folding leaf sight (second type). Lockplate dated 1861. (Maryland-Steuart).

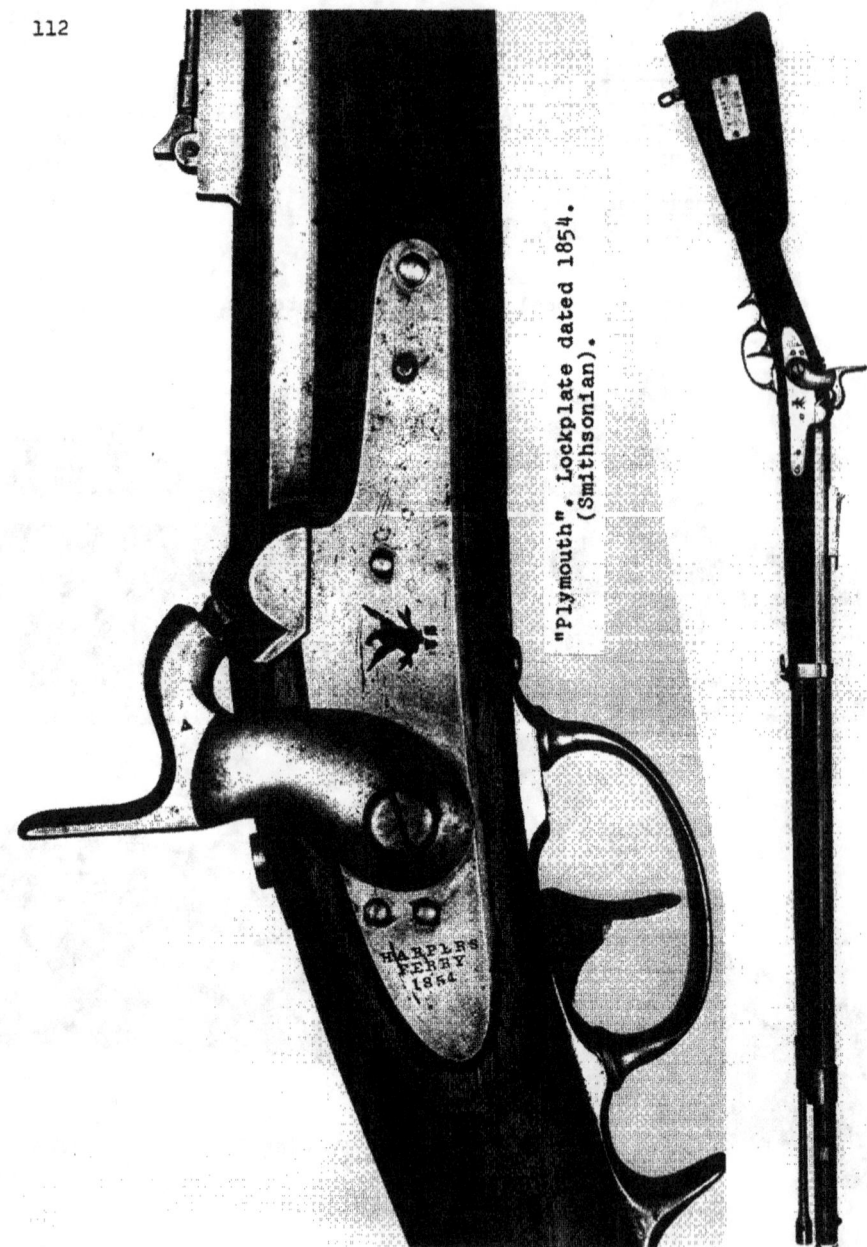

"Plymouth". Lockplate dated 1854. (Smithsonian).

IX. MISCELLANEOUS

Model 1857 Rifle (Navy)

"Plymouth"

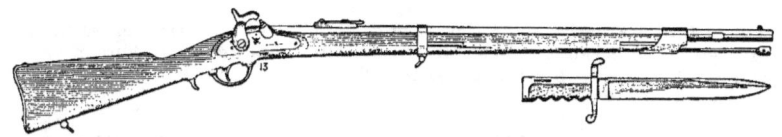

The reduction of the caliber of small arms to .58 did not meet with the approval of Commander John Adolphus Bernard Dahlgren (1809-1870), the head of the Washington (D.C.) Navy Yard, who believed that a larger caliber, heavier projectile was more effective. And, of course, sailors seldom had to carry ammunition.

Dahlgren asked several private contractors to make models, and at least one contractor (Whitney) complied. But Whitney's model did not suit Dahlgren who thereupon had some models made up at the Navy Yard, using as many Model 1842 Musket parts as possible, and including a lock and a stock. The barrel was first turned and bored (to Caliber .69) from a bar of steel, and then it was rifled at Harpers Ferry, the rifling being completed on September 8, 1856.

Meanwhile, Dahlgren ordered from surgical instrument maker Schively of Philadelphia a bowie knife that could be used as a cutlass as well as a bayonet, and on September 17, 1856, Dahlgren submitted his completed rifle to the Navy's Ordnance Bureau.

At about the same period, Dahlgren was given command of the USS Plymouth then being outfitted in Boston to test some heavy Navy ordnance, and on October 10, 1856, Dahlgren asked that 100 of his rifles be made up for trial use aboard the Plymouth. However, the Chief of the Bureau disapproved the Caliber .69, prefering Caliber .58, and it was not until March of 1857, that Dahlgren persuaded the Chief to approve his rifle, and persuaded the Navy Department to allot $2000.00 for 100 of his rifles that were to be made up at Harpers Ferry.

However, Harpers Ferry then had its hands full tooling up for the 1855 Series, and the probabilities are that Dahlgren's rifles were not made entirely at Harpers Ferry - - - on February 17, 1858, Dahlgren asked the Chief of the Bureau for permission to send some barrels to Harpers Ferry for rifling; the Chief asked that Harpers Ferry do the rifling; and the probabilities seem to be that the rifling was done at Harpers Ferry.

What is apparently one of Dahlgren's models, lockplate dated 1854, is in the Smithsonian (see page 112).

The barrel is 34 in. long, and it is equipped with a long range peep sight. Its only marking, other than those on the lockplate, is the arm's weight "9.84" stamped on the trigger guard.

Lewis' collection includes another specimen with an 1854 dated lockplate.

Another specimen is reported, with the barrel stamped, in three lines, "Plymouths Pattern 1858", and with an 1855 dated Harpers Ferry lockplate. Otherwise this specimen is the same as the Smithsonian specimen.

By 1861, Dahlgren had become the Navy's most prominent ordnance officer, and in that year, Whitney was given an order to produce 3000 of Dahlgren's rifles. These rifles, in addition to being called "Plymouths", are sometime called "Whitneyvilles" and "Dahlgren Rifles", and are known officially as the Model 1861 Rifle (Navy).

References:

    Hay, "The Plymouth Rifle".
    Hay, "More on the Plymouth Rifle".
    Fuller, The Rifled Musket 254.
    Pike, "The Plymouth Rifle".

Rampart Rifles

Sawyer states that, in 1806 and 1807, "and probably also before and after", Harpers Ferry made heavy rampart rifles with bores that ranged in size from one that could accomodate a 3/4 in. ball to one that could accomodate a 1 3/4 in. ball. The arms weighed "from 20 pounds upward", and were "used principally on the ramparts of wooden forts scattered along the frontier".

Sawyer refers to one flintlock rampart rifle with a rear sight that was adjustable both horizontally and vertically, and that was held by set screws. (1)

Harpoon Guns

In 1811, according to the Bomford production records, Harpers Ferry produced four "harpoon guns", and in 1813, according to the *Cartridge*, Harpers Ferry produced forty "harpoon guns".

But why would Harpers Ferry produce harpoon guns?

One whaling authority advises that, prior to 1850, the only harpoon guns in general use were the Scotch blunderbuss, invented in 1731, and the English Greener gun invented in 1771. (2) The former weighed eighty pounds, and had a 1 3/4 in. bore, and the latter weighed fifty-five pounds, and had a 1 1/2 in. bore. The harpoons used in these early guns varied in weight from five to nine pounds. Another whaling authority states that the Greener, a swivel gun, could throw a harpoon and attached line perhaps as much as 100 feet, but could not be used effectively unless the sea was very calm. He also states that American "whalemen used them almost not at all except in the protected California bays". (3)

The answer as to why Harpers Ferry produced harpoon guns is probably Robert Fulton's torpedoes and Robert Fulton's torpedoes may have been the reason for the production of other early Harpers Ferry "wall pieces".

Robert Fulton (1765-1815), a Pennsylvania-born painter-engineer, was living in Paris at the turn of the 19th Century when he invented several secret and destructive naval weapons, it being his belief that such weapons would do away with Naval warfare - - - the title page of one of Fulton's later writings contains the motto "The Liberty of the Seas Will be the Happiness of the Earth". (4)

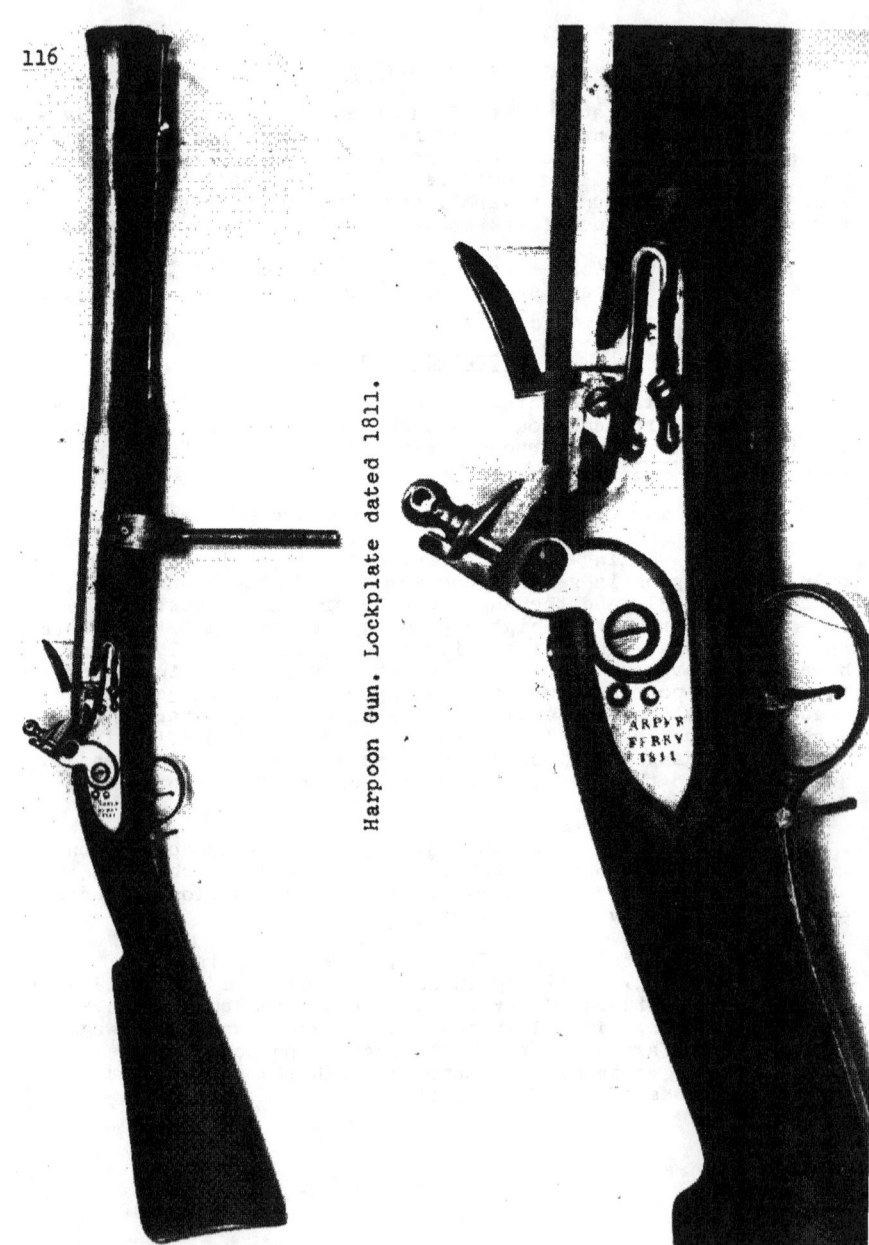

Harpoon Gun. Lockplate dated 1811.

One of Fulton's weapons was a submarine, another was a contact mine (Fulton called it a torpedo), and a third was what Fulton called a clock-work torpedo.

In France, in 1801, Fulton construced the <u>Nautilus</u>, a submarine that may well have been the genesis of Jules Verne's fictional <u>Nautilus</u>. And in 1804 and 1805, during the blockade of Boulogne, the French tried Fulton's torpedoes against British ships of war, but because of minor difficulties, the torpedoes were not successful.

Napoleon was primarily interested in land warfare, and Fulton, discouraged by lack of interest on the part of the French, as well as on the part of the Dutch ambassador to Paris, took his ideas to London where William Pitt, England's Prime Minister, thought well enough of Fulton's clock-work torpedo to sponsor a test.

The clock-work torpedo consisted of a semi-buoyant, water-tight "copper case, containing one hundred pounds or more of gunpowder", and attached to the case was "a cylindrical brass box * * * in which is a gun lock, with a barrel two inches long to receive a charge of powder and a wad" and in the brass box, there was also "a piece of clock-work * * * which being wound up and set, will let the lock strike fire in any number of minutes which may be determined, within an hour".

In theory, the torpedo, its clock-work set, would be thrown overboard; the tide would carry it to a point directly beneath a moored enemy vessel; and the clock-work mechanism would detonate the torpedo, destroying the enemy vessel.

On October 15, 1805, a Fulton clock-work torpedo, containing 180 lbs. of gunpowder, and set to explode in 18 minutes, floated down-tide and literally blew out of the water the test target, and old Danish brig named the <u>Dorothea</u>.

However, the sea-powerful British possessed ample, more conventional means of destroying enemy vessels, and Fulton set sail for the United States where he hoped to interest his own government in his "torpedo war" inventions.

Fulton arrived in New York on December 13, 1806, and the next month, in Washington, he was received by Secretary of State James Madison and by the Secretary of the Navy. A government appropriation was authorized, and in July of 1807, in New York harbor, Fulton's torpedoes were tested against a 200 ton brig. In the first attempt, the tide took the torpedoes "under the brig near her keel, but in consequence of the locks turning downwards, the powder fell out of the pans and they both missed fire". On the second attempt, the torpedo exploded, but not beneath the brig. On the third attempt, the brig was blown up - - - "nothing was seen in the place of the vessel but a high collum of water, smoke, and fragments". (5)

Next, Fulton hit upon an idea not only to make certain that his torpedoes exploded beneath rather than beside a moored vessel, but also to make it possible to use his torpedoes against a vessel that was underway.

This improvement of the clock-work torpedo involved the use of a harpoon, and of a swivel harpoon gun mounted on the stern sheets of a small, twelve man boat. A short length of line was attached to an eye on the aft end of the harpoon, with the other end of the line being attached to the torpedo. The harpoon would be fired into the bow of an enemy vessel, and the torpedo, its clock-work set, would be thrown overboard. The movement of the enemy vessel (if it was underway) or the movement of the tide (if the enemy vessel was moored) would bring the torpedo directly beneath the enemy vessel, at about midships, the line attached to the harpoon and to the torpedo being of an appropriate length, and when the clock-work mechanism detonated the torpedo, the enemy vessel would be destroyed.

By letter dated November 7, 1807, Secretary of War Henry Dearborn directed James Stubblefield, the Superintendent at Harpers Ferry to make up a gun according to a sketch that he enclosed with his letter, and according to the following specifications: - - - the "work is to be done very strong, but need not be highly polished. A common musket lock will answer. The barrel should be made thicker so as to bear high proof.

"The swivel should be made strong enough to support a very heavy charge without giving in any part. The breech of the stock should be strong and about the ususal length of that of a musket * * * let the pivot of the swivel be about 4 1/2 inches long, and when you prove the gun, let the pivot be put into an auger hole in a piece of timber, so as to try its strength, as well as the strength of the gun".

It does not seem unreasonable to conclude that this gun was intended to be used in additional Fulton clock-work torpedo experiments.

By letter dated December 23, 1807, addressed to Stubblefield, Dearborn acknowledged receipt of "the wall piece mentioned in your letter of the 19th inst." (6)

A wall piece, as the name implies, was intended to be fired from a wall, rampart or other fortification, or from a gunwhale of a ship or boat, and the secret nature of Fulton's clock-torpedo experiments may well have persuaded Dearborn to refer to the gun as a wall piece rather than as a harpoon gun.

An 1807 dated Harpers Ferry "wall piece", acquired in England, is in the collection of John McMurray. (7)

It is of interest to note that the authors of the article conclude that the McMurray gun's "short, smoothbore barrel, heavy and cannon-like, was clearly not meant for long-range fire. The sights are also a short-range proposition. Evidently the gun was expected to deliver a tremendous smashing force at short range - - - it seems that the Harpers Ferry wall piece was not intended to be an anti-personnel weapon".

It seems reasonable to conclude that the McMurray gun, marked with the serial number 2, is either the gun received by Dearborn on December 23, 1807, or an armory duplicate.

By his letter, Dearborn also requested Stubblefield to "have six more made; and to add to sight near the middle and instead of the pins to secure the stock to the barrel, to add another gripe or hoop".

Dearborn acknowledged receipt of the "six wall pieces" by letter dated August 1, 1808.

There is an 1808 dated specimen in the Fuller Collection, with all parts marked "5". It does not appear ever to have been equipped with a swivel.

Peterson labels the Fuller specimen "spurious", (7a), but does not offer any explanation. The specimen's lockplate has the shape and markings of lockplates generally found on arms of a later date but even so, the term "spurious" might be too strong.

In January of 1810, at "Kalorama", the Washington residence of Fulton's friend and benefactor Joel Barlow, Fulton exhibited and explained his improved clock-work torpedo plans to President Jefferson, Secretary of State James Madison, and a large number of Members of Congress. Also in Washington, on February 17th, Fulton delivered a lecture on his clock-work torpedo, and then exhibited, among other things, a "harpooning gun".

To test the gun, Fulton had fired harpoons, fifteen or twenty times, from thirty to forty feet, at a target six feet square, never missing, and driving the barbed point of the harpoon through three inch boards "up to the eye" (of the harpoon).

Fulton's proposed torpedo boats would be 27 feet long, and would be propelled by six "long oars" each manned by one oarsman. In addition to a harpoon gun, each boat would be equipped with four swivel blunderbusses (one mounted on each bow, and one mounted on each quarter) that would fire cartridges containing twelve half-ounce balls. Each of the blunderbusses would be manned by a marine, also armed with a "horse-pistol" and a cutlass. Each of the six oarsmen would be armed with a cutlass. And in addition to the oarsmen and marines, each boat would carry one harpooner and one bowman.

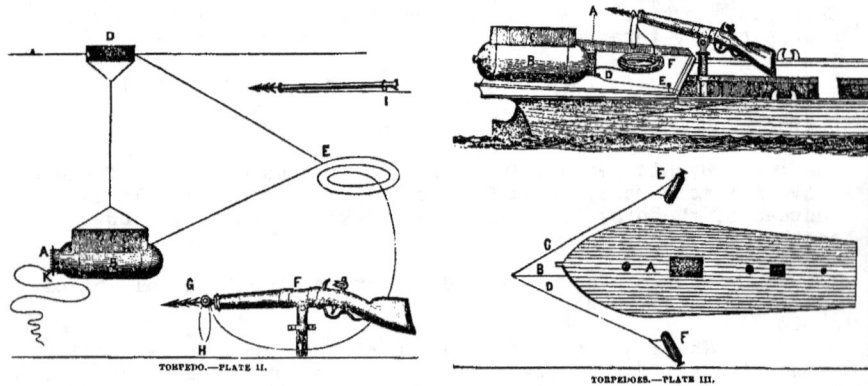

TORPEDO.—PLATE II.   TORPEDOES.—PLATE III.

Fulton proposed that flotillas of fifty torpedo boats would attack at night, with twenty-five torpedo boats attacking an enemy's vessel on the enemy's larboard bow, and twenty-five attacking on the enemy's starboard bow. In answer to objections that the torpedo boats "would be explosed to grape, cannister, and musket balls" from the enemy vessel, Fulton estimated the time of danger to not exceed four minutes - - - two in approaching near enough to fire the harpoon, and two for retreating. And Fulton pointed out that the explosion of only one torpedo would sink a ship.

For experiments, Fulton asked appropriations for six torpedoes, two boats, and two harpoon guns.

The officials in Washington were impressed, and in March, Congress appropriated $5000.00 to be expended under the direction of the Secretary of the Navy. New York Harbor was selected for the test site, and the test target was to be the sloop-of-war <u>Argus</u>, commanded by the "gallant Captain Lawrence".

However, the Navy saw to it that the *Argus* was equipped with a protective net and other elaborate devices designed to guard against Fulton's weapon, whereas Fulton, deprived of all of the advantages of surprise, was left with little more than "one torpedo and eight bad oarsmen". Moreover, the harpoon "did not take effect at so great a distance as (Fulton) supposed it would do", and the experiment was a failure. (8)

There is a harpoon gun, 1810 dated lockplate, in the Nunnemacher Collection (see page 122) that has an eliptical muzzle, a 26 1/2 in. barrel, pin fastened, and is marked with a Navy anchor. The barrel does not have the customary proof marks.

An 1811 dated specimen (see page 116) was on exhibition at the Philadelphia Centennial (1876), but the present whereabouts of the gun is not known.

When war was declared in 1812, Fulton revived his torpedo schemes. On March 1, 1813, from New York where he was "expecting the enemy", Fulton wrote: "I have not been idle, I have prepared 9 torpedoes with locks that strike fire by concussion, and four with clockwork locks". Fulton planned to drive the enemy from the waters of New York, and he expressed regret that he did not have enough torpedoes for the Chesapeake. (9)

Harpers Ferry made forty harpoon guns in 1813.

Lossing states that "while they (Fulton's torpedoes) were not actually used, except in a few isolated cases, against the British vessels of war, a wholesome fear of them was abroad in the British Navy. There was great anxiety manifested on the part of the British Naval commanders, when they approached our coast, to know where Mr. Fulton was; and, such was their caution, they seldom attempted to enter the harbors of the United States during the war. No doubt the fear of Fulton's torpedoes saved several of our sea-port towns from destruction". (10)

Would Fulton's torpedoes have saved Washington?

- - - - - - - - - - - - - - - - - -

Both the McMurray specimen and the Fuller Collection specimen have eliptical muzzles that measure 3 in. (horizontal) by 2 in., and Van Rensselear lists a "flintlock blunderbuss, 3-inch elliptic muzzle, length 35 inches; another dated 1821". (11)

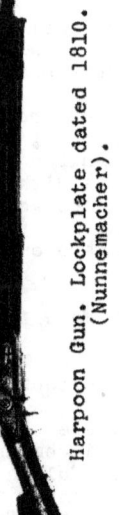

Harpoon Gun. Lockplate dated 1808. (Fuller No. 690).

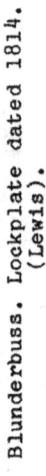

Harpoon Gun. Lockplate dated 1810. (Nunnemacher).

Blunderbuss. Lockplate dated 1814. (Lewis).

Was the eliptical muzzle intended to hold the flat head of the harpoon so that it would pierce the side of the ship with the grain which, of course, ran horizontally, rather than across the grain?

It seems reasonable to conclude that Harpers Ferry's harpoon guns were made to be used with Fulton's clock-work torpedoes.

Fulton's design called for a harpoon with a round iron shank, one-half inch in diameter, two feet long, and with a one inch butt, "the exact calibre of the gun from which it is to be projected".

Both the McMurray and the Fuller specimens are smooth-bore, and have 1 in. bores. The McMurray barrel is 25 in. long while the Fuller barrel is 27 3/4 in. long. The sling swivels on the two arms are similar.

The McMurray is 41 3/4 in. overall; the Fuller is 43 in. overall. The McMurray weighs 24 3/4 lbs.; the Fuller weighs 9 1/2 lbs.

The McMurray lockplate is marked with "U.S." in script, a spread eagle, Harpers Ferry, and the date. The stock measures 17 in. from the butt to the rear end of the barrel, and the pintle is 5 1/2 in. long. The barrel is marked "2" immediately in front of the proof marks (that are the same type as those found on Model 1805 Pistols), and there is an oval sight on the breech tang. The Fuller specimen does not have the usual proof marks on the barrel.

The Fuller lockplate is 6 1/4 in. by 1 1/4 in. The iron pan is detachable. The half octagonal barrel measures 1 3/4 in. across the square at the breech. The two ramrod pipes are brass, and the side plate is brass. Otherwise, the furniture is iron. The trigger guard is "the typical 1795 type" with pointed straps.

Blunderbusses

<u>Note</u>: The word "blunderbuss" is believed to have derived from the Dutch "donderbuss" ("thunder gun"). A blunderbuss, when fired, is held in the hands (or hand) rather than being mounted on a swivel.

Some years ago, Colonel B. R. Lewis acquired a Harpers Ferry blunderbuss from an old Military Academy in Venezuela. He describes this 20 3/4 in. overall specimen, 1814 dated lockplate, as the "short-stocked one-hand type", and expresses the opinion that it was intended "for use in rigging or other precarious positions". (12)

According to Lewis, the United States, in the early 1820's, sent to Venezuela, to aid that country in its efforts to free itself from Spain, a "few" blunderbusses and "quite a number" of Springfield Model 1822 Muskets. Lewis writes that the muskets were dated 1820, 1821 and 1822, and that these arms transfers "were authorized by Congress in closed session as we could not afford to get in trouble with Spain". Finally, Lewis states that "the Venezuelans needed a lot of short firearms for their 'cowboy' mounted troops from the Llanos, led by (Jose Antonio) Paez" (1790-1873), and used the Harpers Ferry blunderbusses as models, cutting down "a lot of the muskets to the same dimensions, flaring out the muzzles at local blacksmith shops, and cutting down the stocks". Finally, Lewis observes that "we must have sent a substantial part of the early M 1822 production, as these dates are very rare here, but the prevailing ones on muskets found in Venezuela".

Lewis further states that "a small number of blunderbusses were made for our Navy during the War of 1812" and that "they specified British sea service style mounts, as the bronze was better for sea service".

Lewis states that his blunderbuss has "British style mountings rather crudely done", that "the frizzen spring is not original, though from a similar HF lock" and that "there is an eagle head on the barrel and several 'V' marks on interior parts".

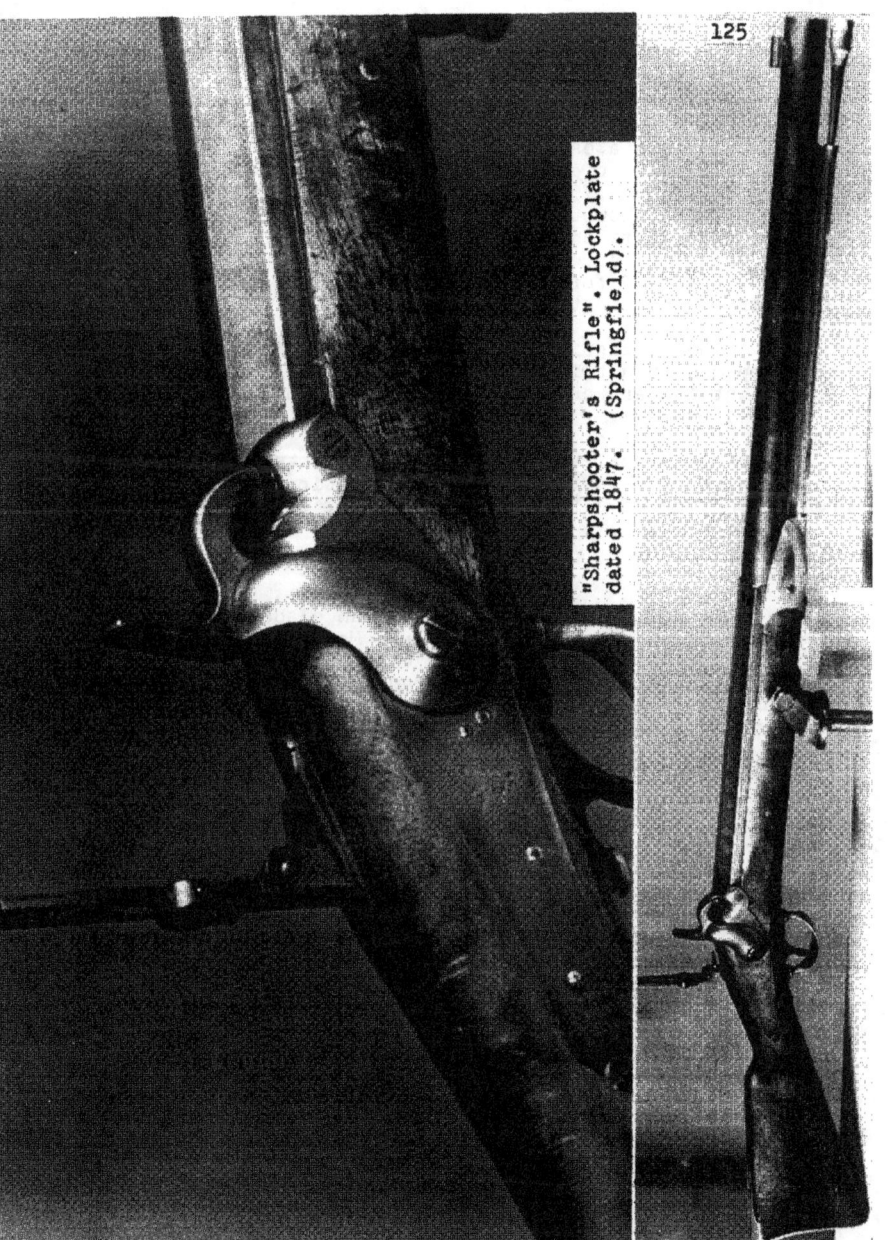

"Sharpshooter's Rifle". Lockplate dated 1847. (Springfield).

1847 Wall Piece (model)

"Sharpshooter's Rifle"

Lewis states that, in 1847, Harpers Ferry made "four rifle-guns or wall pieces" for use on the western frontier. (13) These were Caliber .75, and were mounted on tripods. The production records show that, in fiscal 1848, Harpers Ferry manufactured two experimental rampart rifles, with stands and appendages. Webster expresses the opinion that these arms were "probably intended for testing and eventual field use either in Mexico or on the frontier". (14)

The Springfield Armory Museum specimen shown herein is equipped with a tripod, is Caliber .75, has a 34 5/8 in. barrel that is part octagonal and part round, and measures 51 1/2 in. overall. (15)

Sawyer calls the arm a "Sharpshooter's Rifle", (16) and Lewis reports that during the Revolutionary War, General Washington ordered a few wall pieces of 2 oz. Caliber for long range sniping. (17)

Presentation Pieces

A dealer's catalogue lists "an elaborate and beautiful presentation decorated" Harpers Ferry Model 1816 Musket, with lockplate dated 1822, and states "that similar pieces were awarded in the 1830's to the top ranking or No. 1 graduate of both Annapolis and West Point. Gen. Philip Sheridan was the recipient of one from West Point". The gun "was converted before it was engraved and silver mounted". It "is decorated in engraved silver inlays of stars and eagles. There is also a large engraved silver inlay on the cheekpiece side of a flying angel with a trumpet. A large, engraved silver inlay completely surrounds the tang and is almost 4" long. There are three large silver stars on each side of the fore-end. The rib portion of the bbl is engraved and carries in three lines the marking 'N b 14'. Between the breech and the rear band is an engraved or etched design which includes the name F. Reynolds New York. * * * Almost all parts and screws including the bbl. bands are numbered '5'. Iron parts were originally silver plated and much of that finish remains * * * Stock is finely checkered at wrist * * *". (18)

The same dealer, in an earlier catalogue, lists a "Model 1816 Officer's Musket" with Harpers Ferry lockplate dated 1822. The stock is "select wood, checkered at the wrist, and the barrel is engraved in a scroll and leaf design for about 6" forward of the breech plug. A silver nameplate escutcheon is inlet into the wrist just below the tang, and * * * a large and elaborate silver eagle is inlet into the right side of the stock". (19)

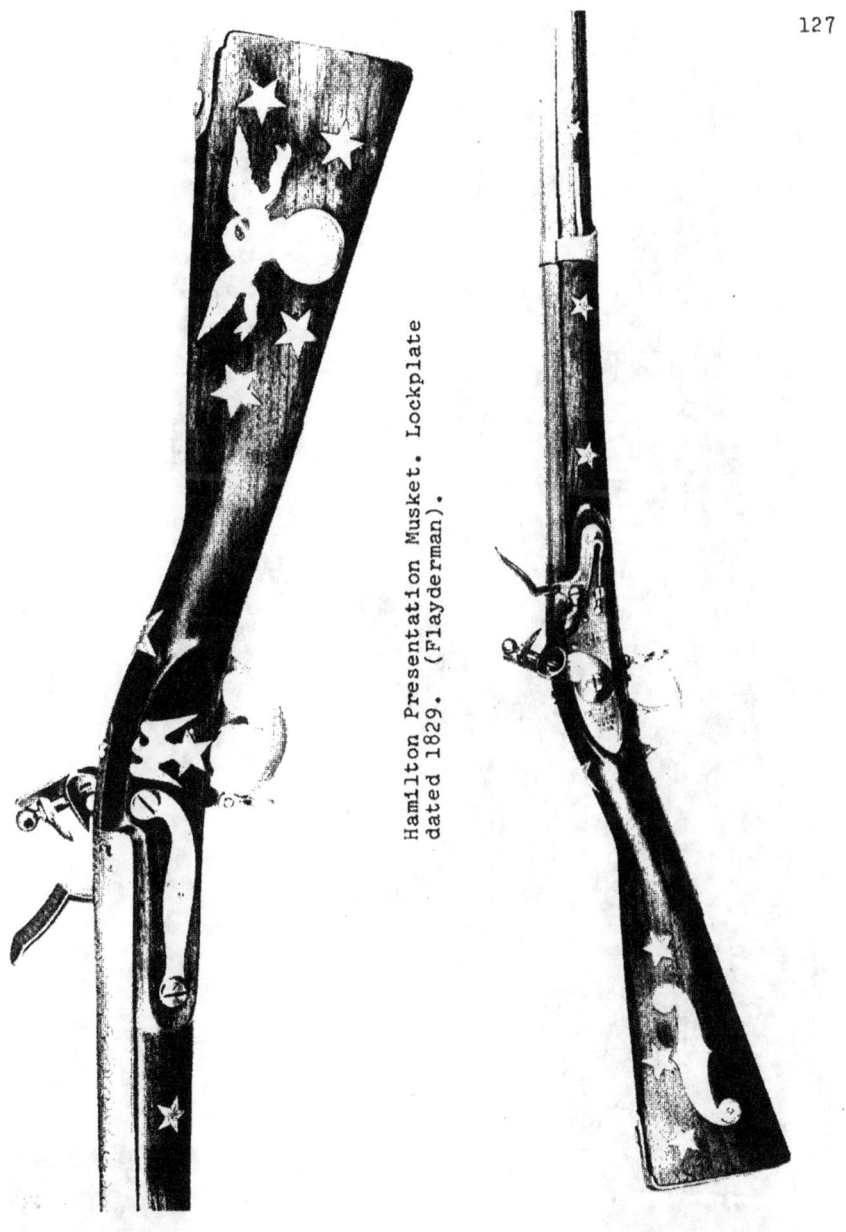

Hamilton Presentation Musket. Lockplate dated 1829. (Flayderman).

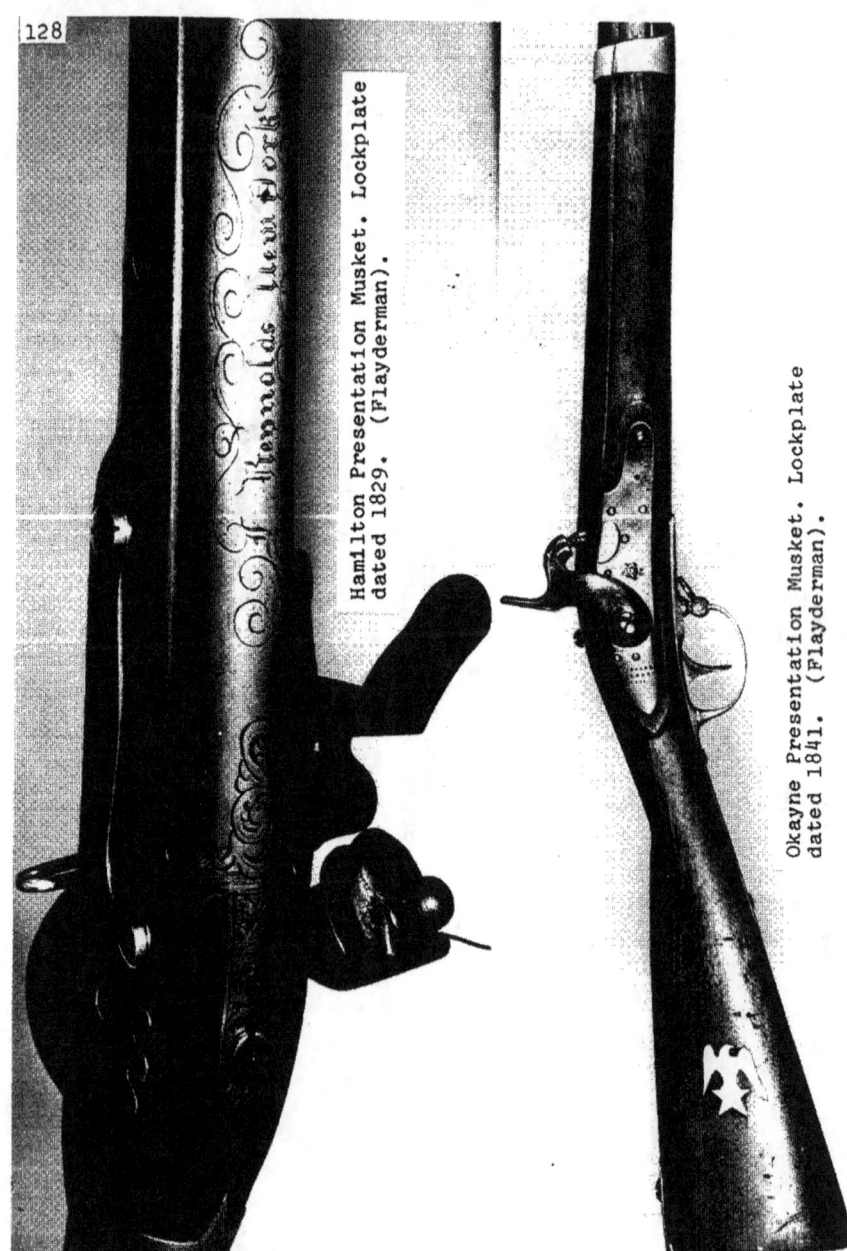

Hamilton Presentation Musket. Lockplate dated 1829. (Flayderman).

Okayne Presentation Musket. Lockplate dated 1841. (Flayderman).

The collection of Norm Flayderman, New Milford, Connecticut, contains a Model 1822 Musket, lockplate dated 1829, with German silver ornamentation by "F. Reynolds New York". See pages 127 and 128. There are, on both sides, two stars between the rear band and the middle band, and two stars between the middle band and the front band. The circular plaque on the left side is inscribed "Presented to Lt. Schuyler Hamilton by his friends at the U. S. Military Academy, June 18, 1845". Hamilton served at West Point as assistant instructor of infantry tactics from November 19, 1844, to June 19, 1845.

The Flayderman collection also contains a musket (converted), 1841 dated lockplate, with less elaborate decoration, but with German silver furniture (instead of iron). See page 128. Its plaque is inscribed "Presented by Captain D. Okane of the Irish volunteers to the company - - August 17, 1854".

Notes

(1) Sawyer 133.
(2) Letter Reginald B. Hegarty to author. January 11, 1968.
(3) Letter Philip F. Purrington to author. January 2, 1968.
(4) Reigart 118.
(5) Ibid. 113, 115 and 116.
(6) Hicks 27.
(7) Patterson and McMurray, "United States Military Wall Guns". This article includes photographs of the arm. (15-2-6 and 15-3-5).
(7a) Peterson, Fuller Collection of American Firearms 55.
(8) Reigart 125, 127 and 130.
(9) Magazine of History with Notes and Queries. Extra No. 35, p. 173.
(10) Lossing, Pictorial Field-Book of the War of 1812. 242-3.
(11) Van Rensselear 111.
(12) Lewis 55. Letter Col. B. R. Lewis to author. March 11, 1968.
(13) Lewis 55.
(14) Webster, "American Wall Guns" 53.
(15) A photograph of the arm mounted on its tripod appears in Patterson and McMurray "United States Military Wall Guns" (15-3-6).
(16) Sawyer 148.
(17) Lewis 55.
(18) Jackson Catalogue 23, Item 701.
(19) Jackson Catalogue 16, Item 235.

Harpers Ferry (Potomac River side) 1857.

X. PRODUCTION RECORDS

The earliest official tabulated Harpers Ferry production records are the 1822 compilation made by Lieutenant Colonel George Bomford, and the 1848 supplement (page 132).

Sawyer classifies these records as "both incomplete and inaccurate", stating that "they exaggerate the number made (at Harpers Ferry) during certain years by incautiously jumbling Model 1800 rifles, Snipper rifles, Wall pieces, Whale Guns, and barrels only which were furnished both to contractors and to militia companies, all in one list. At present there is but one certainty as to their number and that is that it was small. (1)

Additions and corrections to 1822 and 1848 tabulations

(References to Gluckman are to Appendix III)

1801 - Of the 293 muskets produced in 1801, 260 were made between January 1 and September 30, 1801. (2)

Were the remaining 33 produced prior to January 1, 1801, or subsequent to September 30, 1801?

Were the totals for 1801 and other early years computed on a fiscal year basis?

1804 - Gluckman says 161 muskets and 780 rifles.
1806-1808 - For a breakdown on pistol production see page
1807 - Gluckman, Note 2, says 2892 pistols.
1813 - Cartridge also lists 40 harpoon guns.
1815 - Gluckman, Note 3, says 5239 muskets and 1469 rifles.
1818 - Gluckman says 9872 muskets.
1823 - Gluckman says 22 Hall rifles.
1824 - Cartridge says 10557 muskets. Gluckman says 980 Hall rifles.
1828 - Cartridge says 10316 muskets.
1829 - Cartridge says 18895 muskets; Gluckman says 8915 muskets.
1833 - Cartridge says 12040 muskets.
1834 - Cartridge says 12100 muskets.
1835 - Cartridge says 10022 muskets.
1836 - 2 model Hall carbines. Cartridge says 9151 muskets.
1838 - Cartridge says 12006 muskets.
1839 - Cartridge says 5848 muskets.
1840 - Gluckman also lists 3 pattern muskets; Satterlee says 1033 carbines.
1841 - Gluckman also lists 8 pattern rifles; and Satterlee says that the 8650 muskets were "Model 1822's".
1842 - 9 pattern rifles, and 1 model carbine. Cartridge and Satterlee say 6576 muskets; and Satterlee says that the muskets were "Model 1822's".

D.—*Statement of the expenditures at the United States armory at Harper's Ferry, Va., &c.—Continued.*

Arms made and repaired.

Years	Made															Repaired.				
	Muskets	Rifles	Pistols	Pattern muskets	Pattern rifles	Pattern pistols	Wall pieces	Harpoon guns	Torpedo-locks	Torpedo lock-boxes	Cannon-locks	Ball-screws	Screw-drivers	Bullet-molds	Wipers	Rifle-charges	Spring-vices	Muskets	Rifles and carbines	Pistols and swords	Value of repaired arms in new muskets	Total value of arms made and repaired
1796																						
1797																						
1798																						
1799																						
1800																						
1801	293																					
1802	1,472																					
1803	1,048																					
1804	156	772		4	4							772		772	772	772						
1805		1,716										1,716		1,716	1,716	1,716						
1806	136	1,381			8							1,381		1,381	1,381	1,381						
1807	50	146	2,880			1						146		146	146	146		5,500				
1808	3,051		1,208			6																
1809	7,348																	590				
1810	9,400																	691				
1811	10,000					4												1,392				
1812	10,200																	2,113	531	581		
1813	9,000			5	4			40	25									612	231			
1814	10,400	1,600										1,600		1,600	1,600	1,800		548	16			
1815	5,340	1,508										1,508		1,508	1,508	1,508		23	2			
1816	6,416	2,052										2,052		2,052	2,052	2,052						
1817	6,513	2,726		6					6			2,726		2,726	2,726	2,726						
1818	9,892	2,700		8	9							2,700		2,700	2,700	2,700						
1819	7,020	3,324		2	2	6						3,324	12,500	3,324	3,324	3,324						
1820	9,856	1,793										1,793	10,000	1,793	1,793	1,793	3,768					
1821	10,320												8,500				2,266					
Total	119,911	19,718	4,088	30	19	18	7	4	40	25	6	19,718	37,750	19,718	19,718	19,718	6,034	11,469	780	581	$3,208	$15..

NOTE.—In some of the years the expenditures and products of the armory appear to be disproportionate. This has arisen partly by the purchase greater or less quantity of stock and materials in a year than was consumed within it, and partly by the payments of debts in one year which been contracted in the year preceding.

ORDNANCE OFFICE, WAR DEPARTMENT, November 30, 1822.

G. BOMFORD,
Lieutenant Colonel, on Ordnance D

B.—*Statement of expenditures at the United States Armory at Harper's Ferry, &c.—Continued.*

Years	Articles manufactured.												
	Flintlock muskets	Percussion muskets	Rifles	Pistols	Hall's patent rifles	Carbines, Hall's	Ball screws	Wipers	Screw-drivers	Bullet molds	Spring vices	Flint caps	Rifle charges and flasks
From its establishment, in 1796, to—													
31st December, 1821	119,911		19,718	4,088			19,718	19,718	37,750	19,718	6,034		19,718
31st December, 1822	10,000								5,594				
31st December, 1823	12,200								10,343				
31st December, 1824	10,559				1,000			8,173	6,922	1,000			1,000
31st December, 1825	14,000						5,000	11,000	26,928				
31st December, 1826	8,720						5,327	31,827	53,112				
31st December, 1827	12,020				1,000			34,998	8,475		10,100		
31st December, 1828	10,000							25,000	35,679	1,000			1,000
31st December, 1829	8,895								3,653				
31st December, 1830	10,130											51,875	
31st December, 1831	11,160											7,454	
31st December, 1832	12,000				4,360			4,360	4,360	436	436	5,632	20
31st December, 1833	12,000				3,670			19,100	3,682	367	367	17,084	20
31st December, 1834	12,000				970		6,896	22,360	25,941	47	47	5,000	4,734
31st December, 1835	10,000				1,714			1,714	1,714	171	171	2,000	
31st December, 1836	9,150				1,809			1,770	1,770	177	177	10,000	3,000
31st December, 1837	8,200				1,200	1,017	614	17,435	22,809	301	200	70,000	881
31st December, 1838	12,000				2,934		1,136	41,019	25,424	395	1,334	3,000	
30th September, 1839	5,850							22,914	29,000		4,941		
30th September, 1840	8,204				1,023	1,008		10,940	5,202	55	3,418	10,080	
30th September, 1841	8,650				190		1,553	4,428	4,199	25	49	14,817	
30th September, 1842	6,575							14,867	10,685		567	3,234	
30th June, 1843	3,105				300	1,001		1,999	1,950	131	501		
30th June, 1844	608				2,700		73	15,815	3,123	3,191	304		
30th June, 1845		2,225					524	7,472					
30th June, 1846		12,203	*700				478	6,547	8,631	2	1,241		
30th June, 1847		12,000	*3,054				2,747	3,749	19,562	435	3,100		
31st March, 1848	8,200		*2,302				834	7,857	9,908	336	1,019		
Total	336,037	34,628	25,874	4,088	22,870	3,021	45,010	334,562	366,314	27,787	34,006	201,876	30,373

*Percussion.

ORDNANCE OFFICE, Washington, 10th June, 1848.

1843 - 1 musketoon and 1 model percussion rifle. <u>Satterlee</u> says 3108 muskets, and says that they were "Model 1822's".
1844 - <u>Satterlee</u> says that the 608 muskets were "Model 1822's".

After 1844, all arms were percussion.

1845 - 1 model rifle, 2 sets of musket components for private contractors, and 50 sets of rifle components for private contractors. The 2225 muskets were Model 1842's.
1846 - 2 pattern rifles. <u>Satterlee</u> says that the 700 rifles were Model 1841's.
1847 - Of the 12000 muskets, 11600 were complete, and 400 were without bayonets.
1848.- 2 experimental rifled rampart arms, with stands and appendages. The musket total of 8200, and the rifle total of 2202 were for the period ended March 31, 1848. During fiscal 1848, the musket total was 11,000, and the rifle total was 2802.
<u>1849 Fiscal</u> - 8300 muskets, 1925 rifles.
<u>1850 Fiscal</u> - 9600 muskets, 2676 rifles.
<u>1851 Fiscal</u> - 11100 muskets, 3050 rifles.
<u>1852 Fiscal</u> - 13400 muskets, 3227 rifles.

On April 20, 1852, flood waters rose to a depth of ten feet in the yard, and six feet in the shops. No muskets were completed during May or June.

<u>1853 Fiscal</u> - 10101 muskets, 2762 rifles, 9 experimental rifles.
<u>1854 Fiscal</u> - 9000 muskets, 2671 rifles, 1 experimental percussion rifle, 32 balls to the pound. 1 experimental percussion rifle, 22 balls to the pound.
<u>1855 Fiscal</u>   7700 muskets (Model 1842), 1300 rifles, 3 experimental muskets. 590 rifles with long range sights, screw pattern. 449 rifles with long range sights, slide pattern.

During this fiscal year, much altering was done. Also, Harpers Ferry produced the following sword bayonets (for rifles): 1639 with stud attachment, 1646 with ring attachment, and 40 (musician's) with stud attachment. In addition, Harpers Ferry produced 3199 long range rear sights for rifles (screw pattern), and 1662 rear sights for rifles (slide pattern).

<u>1856 Fiscal</u> and <u>1857 Fiscal</u> - During these two years, all of Harpers Ferry's efforts were devoted to altering arms, and to retooling. <u>Satterlee</u> states that 1 model (Model 1855) musket and 2 model (Model 1855) rifles were produced. Davis, <u>U.S. Sword Bayonets</u>, states that Harpers Ferry produced, in 1857, 10 Model 1855 Rifles, and 1 iron mounted Model 1855 Rifle.
<u>1858 Fiscal</u> - 8581 rifle muskets. 374 rifles (Model 1855) complete. 1345 rifles (Model 1855) without long range rear sights.

During this year Harpers Ferry produced 11 brass mounted, brown finished rifles, 1 "with appendages", and 10 apparently without "appendages". (3)

<u>1859 Fiscal</u> - 4400 rifle muskets, complete. 2089 rifle muskets, without bayonets (Fuller, <u>The Rifled Musket</u>, gives the total as 6389). 1500 rifles, without rear sights. 316 rifles, with rear sights. 650 rifles, without rear sights, but with iron mountings.
<u>1860 Fiscal</u> - 5049 rifle muskets. 2300 rifle muskets, with long range rear sights. 190 muskets. 2701 rifles. 1 experimental breech loading cannon. Caliber .48 experimental arms (number not given).
<u>1861</u> - 720 rifle muskets. 420 rifles.

Notes

(1) <u>Sawyer</u> 132.
(2) <u>Gurney</u> 6.
(3) <u>Gun Report</u> Vol. VI, No. 10 (March 1961) p. 4.

Fig. 31.

Fig. 32.

Fig. 33.

THE BURNING OF THE UNITED STATES ARSENAL AT HARPER'S FERRY, by 7 M. APRIL 18, 1861 —[SKETCHED BY D. H. STROTHER.]

The "Large Arsenal" burns, April 18, 1861. An eye witness, David Hunter Strother, walking downhill into Harpers Ferry, reported meeting "a long line of men, women, and boys, carrying loads of muskets, bayonets, and other equipment". Harper's Weekly, May 11, 1861. pp. 292-293.

135

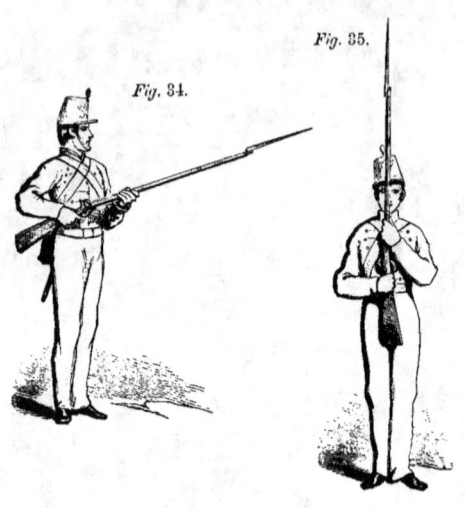

ACKNOWLEDGEMENTS

The author's task was made much easier by the following persons: Richard Adams; Charles Ahalt; Ralph E. Arnold; James A. Bear, Jr., Curator, Thomas Jefferson Memorial Foundation, Incorporated, Monticello; R. H. Bettels; Edwin W. Bitter; Robert Bitter; Trevor Bovee; Stuart E. Brown, III; Walter T. Bruce, Harpers Ferry National Historical Park; Cathryn Childress, Reference Librarian, Mississippi State University; Benjamin H. Davis, Superintendent, Harpers Ferry National Historical Park; Richard H. Dillon, Librarian, Sutro Library, San Francisco; Norm Flayderman; Ralph A. Frederick; Dorrell E. Garrison, Curator, John M. Browning Memorial Museum, Rock Island Arsenal; Samuel Gillully, Director, Montana Historical Society; Craddock R. Goins, Jr., Associate Curator, Division of Military History, United States National Museum, Smithsonian Institution; Raymond W. Gordon; William H. Guthman; Thomas E. Hall, Winchester Museum, Olin Mathieson Chemical Corporation; Virginius C. Hall, Jr., Assistant Director, Virginia Historical Society; J. Garnand Hamilton; Laura D. S. Harrell, Research Assistant, Department of Archives and History, State of Mississippi; Reginald B. Hegarty, Curator, Melville Whaling Room, Free Public Library, New Bedford; Colonel Ed V. Hendren, Jr., The Institute of Heraldry, United States Army; Marvin E. Hoffman, The Museum of Historical Arms; J. Hogan (owner Francis Bannerman Son); Thomas E. Holt;

Donald Jackson, Associate Director and Editor, University of Illinois Press; E. W. Jackson (Jackson Arms); John Melville Jennings, Director, Virginia Historical Society; Curtis C. Jones, Director, Travel Development Division, Department of Commerce, State of West Virginia; Allen P. Karr; Daniel R. Kuehn, Chief Historian, Chickamauga and Chattanooga National Military Park, Fort Oglethorpe, Georgia; Lieutenant Colonel R. C. Kuhn, U.S.A.F.R. (Ret.) (who read portions of the manuscript, and made several significant additions); R. M. Larrick; Ernest D. Laube; John F. Leavitt, Associate Curator, Mystic Seaport; Henry L. Lehmann; Kenneth O. Leonard; Colonel B. R. Lewis, Ordnance Corps, U.S.A. (Ret.) (who read the manuscript, and is responsible for several significant additions); William M. Locke; Andrew F. Lustyik; H. Charles McBarron; Mrs. Stewart McCormack, Curator, Missouri Historical Society; Colonel John H. Magruder III, U.S.M.C.; Arline G. Maver, Curator, Museum & Colt Collection, Connecticut State Library; Charles W. Moore; Maxine Moss, Office Manager, National Muzzle Loading Rifle Association;

Vivien Paladin, Editor, Montana. The Magazine of Western History; C. Meade Patterson; Harold L. Peterson, Chief Curator, National Park Service; Mary Louise Pung, University of California Press; Philip F. Purrington, Curator, Old Dartmouth Historical Society Whaling Museum, New Bedford; Ben B. Quilling;

Glode M. Requa; James C. Roach, Harpers Ferry National Historical
Park; Paul A. Rossi, Director, Thomas Gilcrease Institute of
American History and Art, Tulsa; Henry I. Shaw, Jr., Editor-in-
Chief, <u>Military Collector & Historian</u>; Katherine M. Smith,
Picture Collection, Virginia State Library; Samuel E. Smith
(who read portions of the manuscript, and made several signifi-
cant additions); John Stapleton; Hilda Marie Startzman; Hilda
Staubs, Harpers Ferry National Historical Park; Chan Stith,
Associate Editor, <u>The American Rifleman</u>; Colonel Gerald C.
Stowe, Curator, West Point Museum; William E. Swanson, Sr.
(Elmer Swanson); Thomas Wallace, Museum Curator, Springfield
Armory Museum; N. E. Warriner, Virginia Historical Society;
Donald L. Whipp, Editor, <u>Valleys of History</u>, The Potomac Edison
Company; and Eldon G. Wolff, Curator of History, Milwaukee
Public Museum.

    Also, Charles J. Affleck of Winchester, Virginia.

ILLUSTRATIONS CREDITS

Charles J. Affleck - 26

Charles Ahalt - 24 (top)

Ralph E. Arnold - 46, 48, 49, 157 (bottom-2)

Francis Bannerman Son (J. Hogan, Owner). Catalogues 1903 (1960 Reprint), 1938 and 1949 - 13, 57, 65, 72, 78, 93, 97, 103, 107, 109, 113

Edwin W. Bitter - 42, 156

Stuart E. Brown, III - 62

Trevor Bovee - 92 (bottom)

Company of Military Historians - 27, 80

Duane, William. A Hand Book for Infantry. (5th ed.). Philadelphia 1813. - 11, 33, 64

Ralph A. Frederick - 12

Fuller Collection (National Park Service, Chickamauga and Chattanooga National Military Park) - 16, 22 (bottom), 24 (bottom), 63, 66, 82 (top-3), 96, 102, 106, 122 (top)

Thomas Gilcrease Institute of American History and Art - front cover.

Gilham. Manual of Instruction for the Volunteers and Militia - 100, 134, 136, 142, 150

J. Garnand Hamilton - back cover.

Harpers Ferry National Historical Park (National Park Service) - 8, 71, 128, 135

Allen P. Karr - 22 (top)

Henry L. Lehmann - 17, 19, 155 (bottom)

Col. B. R. Lewis - 122 (bottom)

William M. Locke - 54

Lossing. The Pictorial Field-Book of the War of 1812 - 1, 4, 120 123, 138

Andrew F. Lustyik - 82 (bottom)

H. Charles McBarron - 27, 80

Maryland-Steuart. See Virginia State Library.

<u>Nomenclature Descriptive of the Rifle Musket Model 1855</u> - 2

Norton. <u>American Breech-Loading Small Arms</u> - 77

Nunnemacher Collection (Milwaukee Public Museum) - 68, 122(center)

<u>Ordnance Manual</u> (1841) - 83, 90, 140

<u>Reports of Experiments with Small Arms</u> - 101

Robinson-Pforzheimer Typographical Collection (New York Public Library) - 7, 51, 59, 76, 85, 88, 114, 124

Russell. <u>Guns on the Early Frontiers</u> (University of California Press) - 35

Smith and Swanson. <u>The Antique Pistol Book</u> - 43, 52

Smithsonian Institution - 34, 38, 56, 86, 91, 92 (top), 111 (top), 112, 116, 155 (top)

Springfield Armory Museum - 125

The Institute of Heraldry, United States Army - 51

Virginia State Library. "Virginia State Library. Courtesy Smithsonian Institution" - 74 (top). "Photo by Virginia State Library. From Collections of Virginia Historical Society" (Maryland-Steuart Collection) - 74 (bottom), 111, 157

West Virginia Department of Commerce. Travel Development Division - frontispiece

Winchester Museum - 108

Musket Lock

SHORT-TITLE INDEX

For more information on the longer, identifying titles, see the BIBLIOGRAPHY.

Cartridge - Catalogue of U. S. Cartridge Co. Collection.

Fairbairn and Patterson - Fairbairn and Patterson, "Captain John Hall, Inventor".

Fuller and Steuart - Fuller and Steuart, Firearms of the Confederacy.

Gluckman - Gluckman, Identifying Old U. S. Muskets, Rifles & Carbines.

Gurney - Gurney, "Preliminary Study of the Harpers Ferry Armory and Its Production".

Hicks - Hicks, U. S. Military Firearms 1776-1956.

Hicks (II) - Hicks, Notes on United States Ordnance. Vol. II. Ordnance Correspondence.

Lewis - Lewis, Small Arms and Ammunition in the United States Service.

Metschl - Metschl, The Rudolph J. Nunnemacher Collection of Projectile Arms. Vol. I. Long Arms.

Norton - Norton, American Breech-Loading Small Arms.

Patterson - Patterson, "Harpers Ferry and Its Firearms".

Patterson and Rich - Patterson and Rich, "Civil War Prices of Arms, Parts and Appendages".

Reigart - Reigart, The Life of Robert Fulton.

Russell - Russell, Guns on the Early Frontiers.

Satterlee - Satterlee, A Catalog of Firearms for the Collector.

Sawyer - Sawyer, Firearms in American History. Vol. III. Our Rifles.

Van Rensselear - Van Rensselear, American Firearms.

142

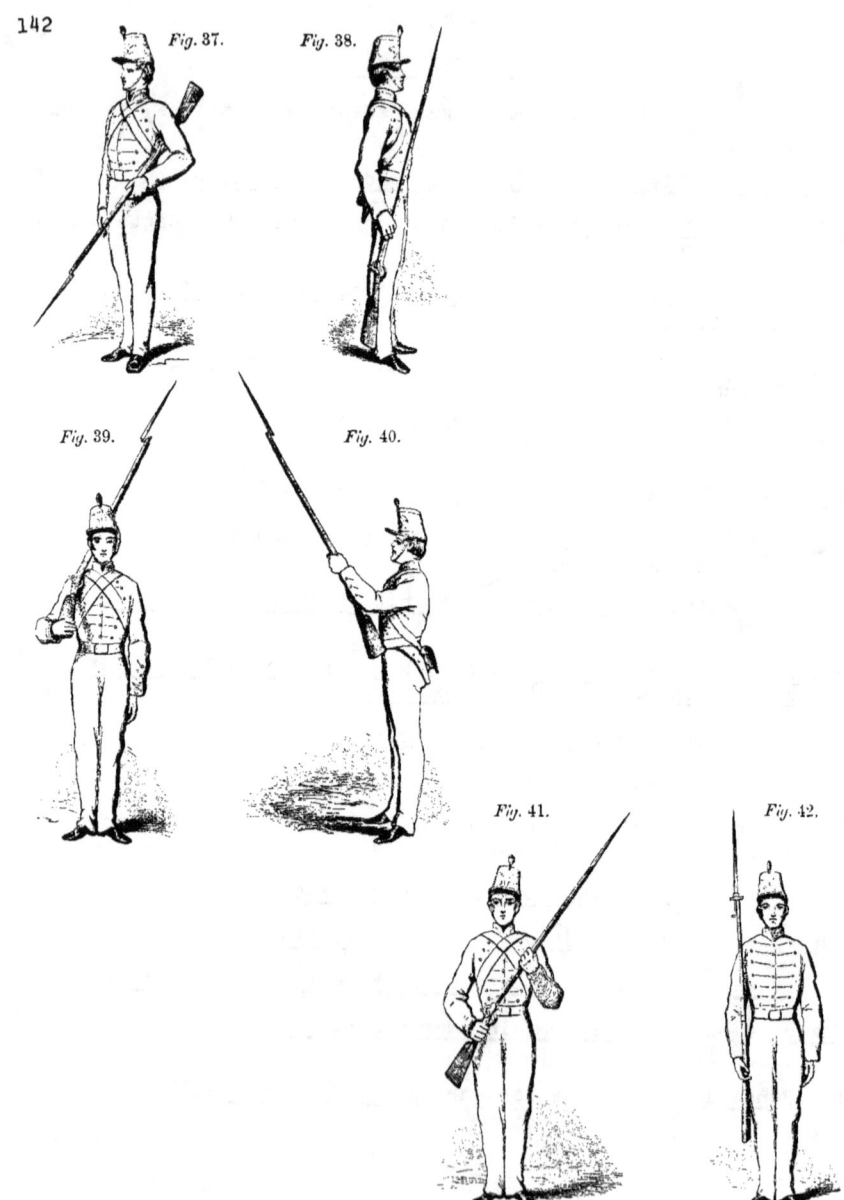

Fig. 37. *Fig. 38.*

Fig. 39. *Fig. 40.*

Fig. 41. *Fig. 42.*

BIBLIOGRAPHY

Printed Books and Pamphlets

Albaugh, William A., III, and Simmons, Edward N. <u>Confederate Arms</u>. Harrisburg 1957.

Andrist, Ralph K. <u>To the Pacific With Lewis and Clark</u>. N.Y. 1967.

Bannerman, David B. <u>Military Goods Catalogue</u>. N.Y. 1855, et seq. (Francis Bannerman Son).

Burrell, Wesley R. <u>Author and Subject Index to the American Rifleman Magazine. 1949-1950</u>. Plainville, Michigan, 1950.

Ditto. <u>1951-1960</u>. Galesburg, Michigan, 1961.

Chapel, Charles Edward. <u>The Gun Collector's Handbook of Values</u>. 7th ed. N.Y. 1966.

Chapel, Charles Edward. <u>Guns of the Old West</u>. N.Y. 1961.

Chapel, Charles Edward. <u>U.S. Martial and Semi-Martial Single-Shot Pistols</u>. N.Y. 1962.

<u>Catalogue of U. S. Cartridge Co. Collection</u>. 1904.

Clark, William. <u>The Field Notes of Captain William Clark, 1803-1805</u>. Ed. by Ernest Staples Osgood. New Haven 1964.

Davis, Rollin V. <u>U. S. Sword Bayonets 1847-1865</u>. Pittsburg 1962. Supplement. 1967.

Dexter, Fred Theodore. <u>Forty-Two Years Scrapbook of Rare Ancient Firearms</u>. Los Angeles 1954.

Dillon, Richard H. <u>Meriwether Lewis</u>. N. Y. 1965.

Duane, William. <u>A Hand Book for Infantry</u>. (5th ed.). Philadelphia 1813.

Fuller, Claud E. <u>The Breech-Loader in the Service</u>. Topeka 1933.

Fuller, Claud E. <u>The Rifled Musket</u>. Harrisburg 1958.

Fuller, Claud E. <u>Springfield Muzzle-loading Shoulder Arms</u>. N.Y. 1930.

Fuller, Claud E. <u>The Whitney Firearms</u>. Huntington, W. Va., 1946.

Fuller, Claud E., and Steuart, Richard D. *Firearms of the Confederacy.* Huntington, W.Va., 1944.

Fulton, Robert. *Concluding Address of Mr. Fulton's Lecture on the Mechanism, Practice and Effect of Torpedoes.* Delivered at Washington February 17, 1810. Washington 1810.

Fulton, Robert. *Torpedo War, and Submarine Explosives.* N.Y. 1810. Reprinted as Extra No. 35. *The Magazine of History with Notes and Queries.* N.Y. 1914.

Gilham, William. *Manual of Instruction for the Volunteers and Militia of the United States.* Philadelphia 1861.

Green, Constance McLaughlin. *Eli Whitney and the Birth of American Technology.* Boston 1956.

Green, Constance McLaughlin. *Washington. Village and Capitol, 1800-1878.* Princeton 1962.

Gluckman, Arcadi. *Identifying Old U. S. Muskets, Rifles & Carbines.* 2d ed. Rev. Harrisburg 1965.

Gluckman, Arcadi. *United States Martial Pistols and Revolvers.* Buffalo 1939. (Reprinted: Harrisburg 1956).

Gun Digest Treasury. The Best from 20 Years of Gun Digest. Ed. by John T. Amber. Chicago 1966. "The Guns of Lewis and Clark" by William R. Barbour. p.6N.

Hardin, Albert Nolan, Jr. *The American Bayonet, 1776-1964.* Philadelphia 1964.

Hasbrouck, Alfred. *Foreign Legionaires in the Liberation of Spanish South America.* N.Y. 1928.

Hicks, James Ernest. *Notes on United States Ordnance.* 2 vols. Mt. Vernon, N. Y., 1940.

The first volume, entitled *Notes on United States Ordnance* Vol. I, *Small Arms* was revised and reprinted in 1946, in 1957, and in 1962 (with the title *U. S. Military Firearms 1776-1956*). The second volume is entitled *Notes on United State Ordnance*, Vol. II, *Ordnance Correspondence*.

Howe, Henry. *Historical Collections of Virginia.* Charleston, S. C., 1845.

Hult, Ruby El. *Guns of the Lewis and Clark Expedition.* Tacoma 1960.

Jackson, Donald, ed. Letters of the Lewis and Clark Expedition with Related Documents 1783-1854. Urbanna, Illinois, 1962.

Jefferson, Thomas. The Papers of Thomas Jefferson. Princeton 1950, et seq.

Kalman, James M., and Patterson, C. Meade. Pictorial History of U. S. Single-Shot Martial Pistols. N.Y. 1957.

Koller, Lawrence R. Fireside Book of Guns. N. Y. 1957

Lewis, Berkeley R. Small Arms and Ammunition in the United States Service. Washington 1956.

Lewis, Meriwether, and Clark, William. History of the Expedition Under the Command of Lewis and Clark, etc. Ed. by Elliott Coues. 4 vols. N. Y. 1893.

Lewis, Meriwether, and Clark, William. Original Journals of the Lewis and Clark Expedition. Ed. by Reuben Gold Thwaites. 8 vols. N. Y. 1904-1905.

Lossing, Benson John. The Pictorial Field-Book of the War of 1812. N. Y. 1868.

Lustyik, Andrew F. Civil War Carbines. Aledo, Illinois, 1962.

Metschl, John. The Rudolph J. Nunnemacher Collection of Projectile Arms. Vol. I. Long Arms. Milwaukee Public Museum Bulletin Vol. 9. Milwaukee 1928.

Mirsky, Jeannette, and Nevins, Allen. The World of Eli Whitney. N. Y. 1952.

Norton, Charles B. American Breech-Loading Small Arms. N. Y. 1872.

The Ordnance Manual for the Use of the Officers of the Confederate States Army. Richmond 1863.

Ordnance Manual for the Use of the Officers of the United States Army. Washington 1841.

Ordnance Manual for the Use of the Officers of the United States Army. 2d ed. Washington 1850.

Peterson, Harold L. The Fuller Collection of American Firearms. 1967.

Peterson, Harold L. Pageant of the Gun. Garden City 1967.

Peterson, Harold L. *The Treasury of the Gun.* N. Y. 1962.

Regulations for the Government of the Ordnance Department. 1st May 1834. Washington 1834.

Regulations for the Inspection of Small Arms. Washington 1823.

Reigart, John Franklin. *The Life of Robert Fulton.* Philadelphia 1856.

Reports of Experiments with Small Arms for the Military Service, by Officers of the Ordnance Department, U. S. Army. Washington 1856.

Roberts, Ned H. *The Muzzle-Loading Cap-Lock Rifle.* Manchester, N. H., 1944. Reprinted 1952.

Russell, Carl P. *Guns on the Early Frontiers. A History of Firearms from Colonial Times through the Years of the Western Fur Trade.* Berkeley 1957. Reprinted 1962.

Satterlee, Leroy DeForest. *A Catalog of Firearms for the Collector.* 2d ed. Detroit 1939.

Sawyer, Charles Winthrop. *Firearms in American History, 1600 to 1800.* Boston 1910.

Sawyer, Charles Winthrop. *Firearms in American History.* Vol. III. *Our Rifles.* Boston 1921. Reprinted 1941 and 1946.

Sawyer, Charles Winthrop. *United States Single-Shot Martial Pistols.* Boston 1913.

Serven, James Edsall, ed. *The Collecting of Guns.* Harrisburg 1964.

Shields, Joseph W. *From Flintlock to M-1.* N. Y. 1954.

Smith, James A., and Swanson, Elmer. *The Antique Pistol Book.* Hoboken 1948.

Smith, Winston O. *The Sharps Rifle.* N.Y. 1943.

Sutcliffe, Alice Crary. *Robert Fulton and the "Clermont".* N. Y. 1909.

Van Rensselear, Stephen. *American Firearms. A Histology of American Gunsmiths, Arms Manufacturers & Patentees with Detailed Descriptions of Their Arms.* Watkins Glen. N. Y., 1947.

Wasson, Robert Gordon. *The Hall Carbine Affair*. N. Y. 1941. Reprinted 1948.

Webster, Donald B., Jr. *American Socket Bayonets 1717-1873*.

West Virginia. A Guide to the Mountain State. N. Y. 1941.

Winant, Lewis. *Early Percussion Firearms*. N. Y. 1959.

Magazine Articles, etc.

The American Rifleman December 1955, p. 84; June 1959 p. 20; and August 1962, p. 19.

Arnold, Ralph E. "A Pair of Harpers Ferry Pistols". *Gun Report* Vol. XIII, No. 8 (January 1968) p. 8.

Cochran, Keith. "American Firearms Publications 1885-1964". *Gun Report* Vol. XII, No. 5. (October 1966), p. 28.

Crocker, Justin S. "U. S. Model 1842 Musket". *Gun Report* Vol. XII, No. 4 (September 1966) p. 24.

Fairbairn, Charlotte Judd, and Patterson, C. Meade. "Captain John Hall, Inventor". *Gun Report* Vol. V, No. 5 (October 1959) p. 6, et seq.

Fuller, Claud E. "The Harpers Ferry Armory". *Texas Gun Collector* No. 50 (September 1954) p. 5.

Gun Collector Vol. 33, p. 461.

Gun Collector Letter 1-2. Madison, Wisconsin, 1946.

Gun Report Vol. III, No. 6 (November 1957) p. 4; Vol. III, No. 12 (May 1958) pp. 27 and 65; Vol. V, No. 12 (May 1960) p. 4; Vol. VI, No. 10 (March 1961) p. 4; Vol. XI, No. 4 (September 1965) p. 7; Vol. XI, No. 5 (October 1965) pp. 26, 28-30; and Vol. XI, No. 7 (December 1965) p. 67.

Hay, Warren H. "The Plymouth Rifle". *Gun Report* Vol. VIII, No. 2 (July 1962) p. 6.

Hay, Warren H. "More on the Plymouth Rifle". *Gun Report* Vol. X, No. 8 (January 1965) p. 8.

Huntington, R. T. "Hall Rifles at Harpers Ferry". *Guns* Vol. VII, No. 4 (April 1961) p. 31.

Kuhn, R. C. "U. S. Small Arms Inspectors". *The American Rifleman* December 1961, p. 66 Supplement. *The American Rifleman* October 1964, p. 107.

Lewis, Berkeley R. "Older Service Weapons Given Wrong Designation". *Gun Report* Vol. XII, No. 3 (August 1966) p. 47.

Lord, Francis A. "The Mississippi Rifle". *Civil War Times Illustrated* Vol. 3 (February 1965) pp. 36-38.

Lustyik, Andrew F. "Civil War Carbines". *Gun Report* Vol. VII, No. 3 (August 1961) p. 6.

The Magazine of History with Notes and Queries. Extra No. 35. N. Y. 1914.

Mitchell, James L. "United States Musket Model 1795". *Antiques* Vol. LI (February 1947) p. 122.

Patterson, C. Meade. "Firearms on the Wilkes Expedition". *Gun Report* Vol. V, No. 3 (August 1959) p. 10.

Patterson, C. Meade. "The Harpers Ferry 1819". *The American Rifleman.* Vol. 97, No. 8 (August 1949) p. 46.

Patterson, C. Meade. "Harpers Ferry and Its Firearms". *The Bulletin of the American Society of Arms Collectors.* No. 11 (Spring 1965) p. 21 et seq.

Patterson, C. Meade, and McMurray, John C. "United States Military Wall Guns". *Muzzle Blasts* Vol. 14, No. 12 (August 1953) pp. 4, 7; Vol. 15, No. 1 (September 1953) pp. 12, 16, 19; Vol. 15, No. 2 (October 1953) pp. 6, 10, 15; and Vol. 15, No. 3 (November 1953) pp. 5-7, 11.

Patterson, C. Meade, and Rich, A. Sheldon. "Civil War Prices of Arms, Parts and Appendages". *Gun Report* Vol. VII, No. 5 (October 1961) p. 6, et seq.

Pike, Edward. "The Plymouth Rifle". *American Arms Collector* Vol. I, No. 2 (April 1957) p. 34.

Russell, Carl P. "The Guns of the Lewis & Clark Expedition". *North Dakota History* Vol. 27, No. 1 (Winter 1960) p. 25.

Smith, Philip R., Jr. "The Harpers Ferry Armory 1796 to 1869". *Gun Report* Vol. VII, No. 11 (April 1962) p. 12.

Smith, Philip R., Jr. "The Hall Rifle Works". *Gun Report* Vol. VII No. 7 (December 1961) p. 26.

The Texas Gun Collector No. 51 (October 1954) p. 18.

Webster, Donald B., Jr. "American Wall Guns". The American
    Rifleman. August 1963, p. 51.

Webster, Donald B., Jr. "The Mississippi Rifle". Gun Report
    Vol. VII, No. 6 (November 1957) p. 6.

Weller, Jac. "Flintlock to Percussion Rifle". Ordnance
    Vol. XXXVI, No. 195, p. 446.

Typescripts and Manuscripts

"Annual Production Data, Arms and Tools and Expenditures at the
    United States Armory at Harper's Ferry, Va., 1796-1860".

Gurney, Hugh D. "Preliminary Study of the Harpers Ferry Armory
    and Its Production". February 15, 1965.

Sawyer, Charles Winthrop. MSS Notes.

Gun Dealers Catalogues

Abels 32.

Bannerman 1949, 1903 (1960 Reprint), 1938.

Flayderman 79.

Jackson 16, 20, 23, 24.

Kimball 4, 6, 7, 9.

Museum of Historical Arms 15.

2. *Handle* — CARTRIDGE.

One time and one motion.

151. Seize the cartridge with the thumb and next two fingers, and place it between the teeth.

3. *Tear* — CARTRIDGE.

One time and one motion.

152. Tear the paper to the powder, hold the cartridge upright between the thumb and first two fingers, near the top; in this position place it in front of and near the muzzle — the back of the hand to the front.

Fig. 43.

4. *Charge* — CARTRIDGE.

One time and one motion.

153. Empty the powder into the barrel; disengage the ball from the paper with the right hand and the thumb and first two fingers of the left; insert it into the bore, the pointed end uppermost, and press it down with the right thumb; seize the head of the rammer with the thumb and fore-finger of the right hand, the other fingers closed, the elbows near the body.

Fig. 44.

INDEX

Ahalt, Charles 23
Alabama 84
Annapolis. See U. S. Naval Academy.
The Antique Pistol Book 52
Argus (ship) 120, 121
Armstrong, John 37
Arnold, Ralph E. 47
Arsenal Point. See Greenleaf's Point.

Baltimore and Ohio Railroad. Frontis
Barbary pirates 40
Barlow, Joel 119
Barrett, John B. 72
Beckman, Armistead 59
Bell, James 70
Berry, Harry 45
Bitter, Edwin W. 44, 47
Bitter, Robert 44, 47
Black Hawk War 72
Blunderbuss 115, 120, 124
Board of Officers 87
Bomford, George 60, 64, 70, 81, 83, 84, 87, 131
Brady, Richard T. 45, 47
British Navy 121
British sea service style mounts 124
Brown, John 5
Brown, Stuart E., III 68
Buena Vista 93
Burkhart, Mr. 109
Burning of Harpers Ferry 105
Burton, James Henry 101
Butterfield conversion 61

Cannon 134
Carrington, James 70
Charbonneau, Toussaint 33
Charleville. See French Model 1763 Musket.
Chesapeake Bay 121
Chesapeake and Ohio Canal 5
Civil War 72, 98
Clark, Jerome 55
Clark, William 30, 31
Clock-work torpedo 117, 118, 119

Common Rifle 65
Congress 119, 120
Coxe, Tench 18, 20, 21, 36, 37, 44, 51
Craig, Henry Knox 83

Dahlgren, John Aldolphus Bernard 113
Dahlgren Rifle 114
Davis, Jefferson 93, 95, 103, 109
Dearborn, Henry 29, 31, 35, 43, 44, 118, 119
Dorothea (ship) 117
Drewyer 32
Drouillard. See Drewyer.

Enfield Armory 101
Eustis, William 20, 21, 23, 36, 51

Far West Hobby Shop 45
Field, Edward 14
Fillmore, Millard 72
1st Dragoon Regiment 81
1st Infantry Regiment 30, 32
1st Mississippi Regiment 93
First Parish Church (Portland, Maine) 69
Fiscal year basis 44
"Fishtail" lever 79
Flayderman, Norm 129
Flood 93, 133
Florida 81
Floyd, John D. 105
Fort Gibson 81
Fort McNair 41
Fort Monroe 70
France 57, 58
Frederick, Ralph A. 25
French Army 101
French Model 1763 Musket ("Charleville") 13, 14, 18
French Model 1777 Musket 58
French Model 1822 Musket 87
Fuller Collection 25, 64, 76, 83, 88, 89, 119, 121, 123
Fulton, Robert 115, 117, 118, 119, 120, 121, 123

"General issue" 7
Greenleaf's Point 39, 41, 69, 87
Gun Report 55

Hall, John Harris 69, 72, 75, 76, 79, 84, 93
Hall-North Carbine 81
Hamilton, J. Garnand 45
Hamilton, Schuyler 129
Harper, Kenton 109
Harper, Robert 5
Hawkins, Henry 6
Hawthorne, Chauncey 45
Hegarty, Reginald B. 129
Hendren, Ed. V., Jr. 55
Hoffman, Phillip 59
"The Hole" 5
Holt, Thomas E. 41
Huger, Benjamin 84

Indian Wars 40
Ingalls, David L. 45, 55
Irish Volunteers 129
Irvine, Callender 21, 23, 51
"The Island". See Island of Virginius.
Island of Virginius 70

Jackes, J. 8
Jackson, Donald 41
Jackson, Thomas J. "Stonewall" 109
Japan 72, 84
Jay, John 57
Jefferson, Thomas 5, 30, 31, 57, 58, 119
Johnson 55

"Kalorama" 119
Kentucky Rifle 93
Kuhn, R. C. 44, 55

Lancaster (Pennsylvania) 30
"Large Arsenal" Frontis., 8, 135
Lawrence, James 120
Le Blanc 58
Lee, Robert E. 109
Lee, Roswell 39, 57, 58, 64
Lewis, B. R. 6, 39, 65, 79, 85, 87, 88, 90, 124, 126

Lewis, Meriwether 30, 31, 32
Lewis and Clark Expedition 30, 31, 32, 33
Lindner conversion 97
Llanos 124
Locke, William M. 35, 41, 53, 55
Lucie, Dr. James 47

McGuire, Mr. 53
McMurray, John 119, 121, 123
Madison, James 69, 117
Marines 64, 120
Maryland Heights. Frontis.
Maryland-Steuart Collection (Virginia Historical Society) 109
Maynard, George C. 55
Maynard primer 101, 110
Merrill conversion 97, 99
Mexican War 40, 72, 98
Military Police 51
Miller, Robert 97
Minie, C. E. 101
Minnie Ball 95, 98, 101, 104
Moberly (Missouri) 79
"Model" 7
Model Book 6
Model Office 6
Monroe, James 37
Moore, Benjamin 55, 87
"Musket Factory". Frontis, 70
Mutzig Armory 87

"National armory bright" 60
"National armory brown" 60
National Park Service 5
National War College 41
Nautilus (Submarine) 117
Navy 15, 40, 124
Navy Yard (Washington) 113
New York 117, 120, 121
North, Simeon 51, 53, 72, 81, 84
North Model 1811 Pistol 51, 52
North Model 1813 Pistol 51, 52
North Model 1816 Pistol 52
North Model 1819 Pistol 53
Nunnemacher Collection 61, 121

"Officer's Models" 40
Okane, D. 129
Ordnance Board 6, 58, 88, 89, 95
Ordnance Bureau 113
Ordnance Department 60, 87
Ordnance Manual 73
Ordnance Office 6, 99, 101, 104, 107
Ordnance Regulation 1839 (manuscript) 87

Paez, Jose Antonio 124
Partridge, Captain 61
"Pattern" 7
Patterson, C. Meade 14, 29, 41
Pelaux, Peter 21
Perkin, Joseph 10, 29, 31, 35, 43, 44
Perry, Matthew Calbraith 72, 84
Perth (Scotland) 40
Peterson, Harold L. 119
Philadelphia 21, 51, 52
Philadelphia Centennial Exposition 121
Pike, Zebulon Montgomery 32
U.S.S. Plymouth 113
Plymouth Rifle 113, 114
"Porte Crayon". See David Hunter Strother
Portland (Maine) 69
Prescott, Benjamin 57
Pryor, Sergeant 32
Pugsley Collection 28
Purrington, Philip F. 129

Revolutionary War 126
Reynolds, F. 126, 129
Richardson's Wharf (Portland, Maine) 69
"Rifle Works". Frontis, 70, 75, 93, 105
Robb, John 87
Roberts, W. 8
Robertson, W. M. 14
Rock Island Arsenal 73, 78
Russell, Charles M. 33

Sacagawea 33
Sage, Luther 70
St. Louis 32
Schively 113
Schuylkill Arsenal 20, 21
2nd Dragoon Regiment 81
Second Seminole War 81
Secretary of the Navy 117, 120
Seminole War 72
Sharps, Christian 6
Sharps Carbine 5
Sheridan, Philip 126
Shields, John 32
Shoshone Indians 33
Sing Sing Prison 79
Smith, James A. 43, 52
Smith, Samuel E. 44, 45, 47, 52, 55
Smithsonian Institution 40, 58, 59, 88, 114
Snyder, Dr. Thomas B. 45
Springfield Armory 5, 13, 14, 18, 25, 37, 39, 55, 57, 58, 60, 61, 64, 87, 90, 93, 99, 103, 104,
Springfield Armory Museum 90, 126
Springfield Model 1822 Musket 124
Stapleton, John 41
Stocks 9, 37, 39
Strother, David Hunter 7, 135
Stubblefield, James 20, 23, 39, 51, 53, 57, 58, 118, 119
Swanson, Elmer 43, 52

Temple Street (Portland, Maine) 69
Thornton, William 69
Torpedo 115, 123. See, also, Clock-work torpedo.
Torpedo boats 120
26th Infantry Regiment 40

U.S. Military Academy 64, 126, 129
U.S. Naval Academy 126

Van Rensselear, Stephen 52
Vaule, Eric 100
Venezuela 124
Virginia Militia 105, 109
Virginius. See Island of
  Virginius.

Wadsworth, Decius 52, 53, 57,
  58, 60, 61, 65
Wall piece 118, 119
War of 1812 40, 124
Warner, Thomas 87
Washington, George 5, 10, 126
Washington, D. C. 121
Washington, D. C., Arsenal.
  See Greenleaf's Point.
Waters 55

West Indian pirates 40
West Point. See United States
  Military Academy.
Whaling 115
Whiting, John 20
Whitneyville Rifle 114
Whitney, Eli 57, 58, 72, 113
Wickham, Marine T. 21, 23, 51,
  65
Wilkes, Charles 61
Williams, Charles 47
Windsor Rifle 93

Yaeger Rifle 93
Yankee (ship) 69
Yarmouth (Maine) 69

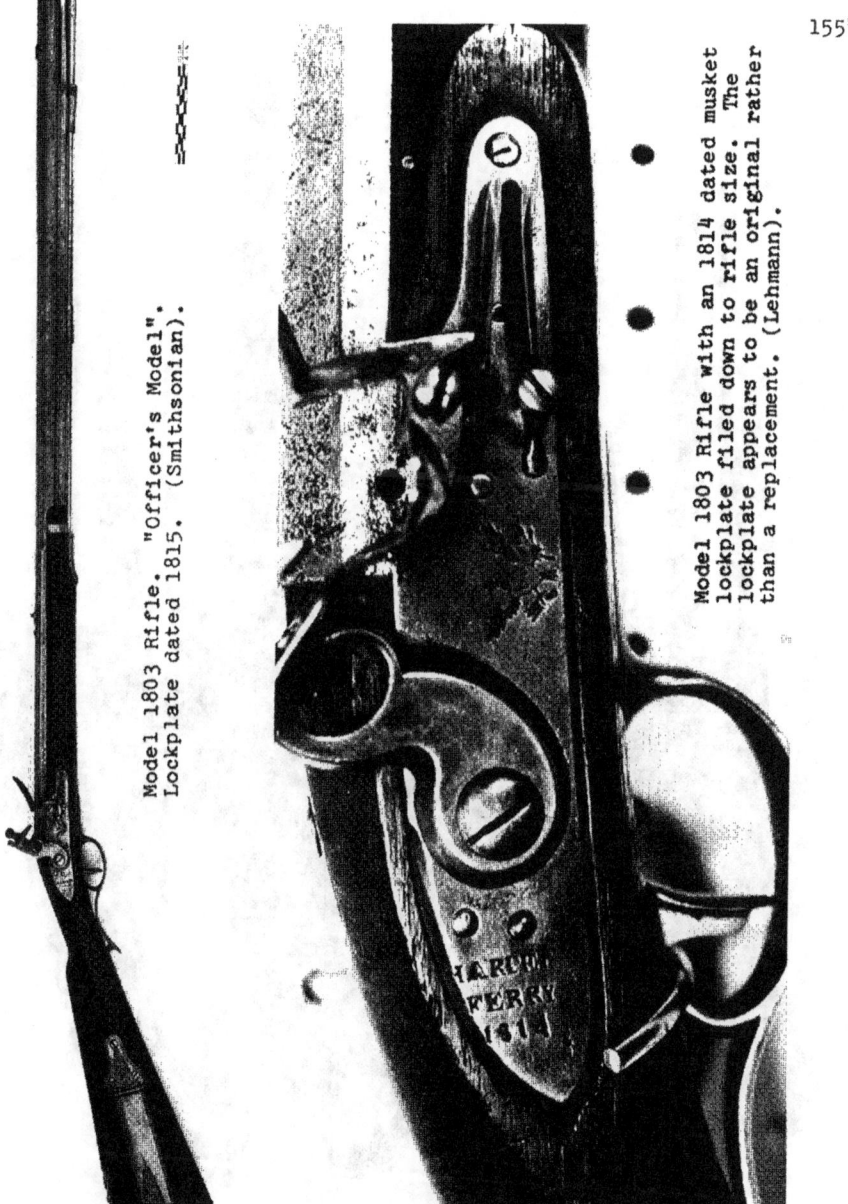

Model 1803 Rifle. "Officer's Model". Lockplate dated 1815. (Smithsonian).

Model 1803 Rifle with an 1814 dated musket lockplate filed down to rifle size. The lockplate appears to be an original rather than a replacement. (Lehmann).

155

Collection of Edwin and Robert Bitter. Lockplates dated (from top to bottom):

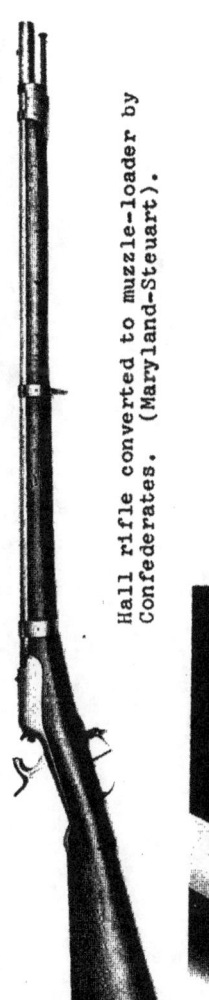

Hall rifle converted to muzzle-loader by Confederates. (Maryland-Steuart).

Model 1806 Pistol. Barrel markings and Inspector's mark. Arnold pair.

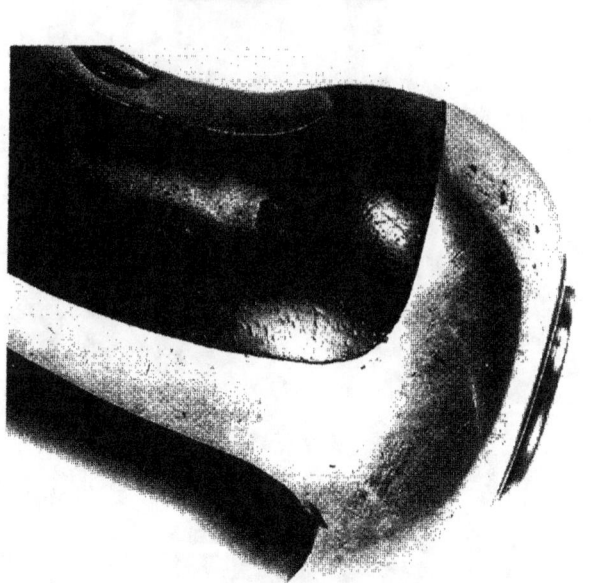

Model 1806 Pistol. Butt markings. Arnold pair.

www.ingramcontent.com/pod-product-compliance
Lightning Source LLC
Chambersburg PA
CBHW052101230426
43662CB00036B/1722